I'm proud to call Reverend Clay Stauffer a treasured personal friend and my spiritual guru. You are about to rediscover what makes a full and complete life. I'm convinced what the world needs now is more teachings from Clay Stauffer!—**Jim Nantz**, CBS Sports & voice of the Masters

Clay Stauffer calls us back home to our common humanity in his book, *What the World Needs Now*. From the very first paragraph, I couldn't put it down. Every person in America should read this book.—**Samar Ali**, research professor of political science and law; co-chair, Vanderbilt Project on Unity & American Democracy

In our era of uncertainty and division, Clay's *What the World Needs Now* gives us a compass of timeless wisdom and spiritual insight that illuminates our shared path forward.—**Bill Frist, MD**, former US Senate majority leader

What the church needs now is practical wisdom, in the manner of Aristotle and Jesus, that encourages virtuous living in these chaotic times. Clay Stauffer has given us a wise, virtuous book full of contemporary, useful guidance for living better lives.—**Will Willimon**, professor of the practice of christian ministry, Duke Divinity School; United Methodist bishop, retired; and author of *Preachers Dare: Speaking for God in the Sermon.*

My good buddy Clay has a new book that I know you will be inspired by. He is a good man with great compassion for his fellow man and blessed with a kind heart. You will enjoy these thoughts on a variety of subjects with which we all struggle.—**Vince Gill**, country music artist

In these thoughtful and insightful reflections, Clay Stauffer gets to the heart of what the world needs now and needs urgently: a renewed focus on character and virtue for all of us. The book is ideal for devotional reading or small-group discussion, and it deserves a wide readership. I heartily recommend it.
—**L. Gregory Jones**, president, Belmont University

I am grateful that Clay is one of the voices striving to remind all of us of the virtues of seeking justice, loving mercy, and walking humbly in a time when loving your neighbor as yourself seems to have gone out of style.—**Bill Haslam**, former governor of Tennessee

One thing that I have always appreciated about Clay Stauffer is that he doesn't shy away from tough questions. In this book, Clay focuses on some of the most important issues facing our troubled world and gives his thoughtful perspective based on his years of experience as a preacher, teacher, scholar, and friend.—**Bill Carpenter**, retired chairman and chief executive officer of Lifepoint Health

As a dad of young boys, it's so encouraging to know there are people like Clay in the world to impart teachings that will shape how they handle the challenges and triumphs of life. I'm proud to call him a friend and advisor. I highly recommend discovering what we all need right now. Let it be your compass for a better life!—**Eric Church**, country music artist

A truly inspiring and timely guide for those seeking balance, purpose, and strength of character in an ever-changing world. A powerful and essential read for the soul.—**John Steele**, president and chief executive officer, Equitable Trust Company

Clay has written a short book of meditations on what truly matters in life. These are the characteristics that define a good life. Read this book slowly. Read it with close friends. Read it with your family. These are the things we must teach again if we are to survive. This is who we must become if we're going to thrive again as humans.—**Mike Glenn**, founder and president, Engage Church Network

Rev. Clay has written a wonderful, timely book that will challenge both young and old, no matter what season of life you may be in. In a day and age where character and virtue seem to be in short supply, Clay shines the spotlight on the core building blocks of living a good, fulfilling life while reminding us that we cannot do it alone. In short, a highly recommended read as a road map to navigate the tricky waters of today's landscape.—**Jay DeMarcus**, Rascal Flatts and chief executive officer of Red Street Records

Clay Stauffer's book gives the rest of us an opportunity to understand the importance of emphasizing character and virtue.—**Lamar Alexander**, former governor of Tennessee; US senator, 2003–2021

In *What the World Needs Now*, pastor-professor Clay Stauffer reminds us that something more powerful than genetics and random life circumstance determine human dignity. That something is choice. While a host of our givens are beyond either choice or control, how one reacts to them determines each person's character. Clay does us a service by reminding us of the priorities that give a life stability in this time of unprecedented moral chaos.—**Rubel Shelly**, teaching minister, Harpeth Hills Church of Christ, Nashville, Tennessee

What the World Needs Now

Virtue and Character in an Age of Chaos

CLAY STAUFFER

Abingdon Press | Nashville

What the World Needs Now

Virtue and Character in an Age of Chaos

Copyright © 2025 Abingdon Press

All rights reserved.

No part of this work may be reproduced or transmitted in any form or by any means, electronic or mechanical, including photocopying and recording, or by any information storage or retrieval system, except as may be expressly permitted by the 1976 Copyright Act, the 1998 Digital Millennium Copyright Act, or in writing from the publisher. Requests for permission can be addressed to Rights and Permissions, The United Methodist Publishing House, 810 12th Avenue South, Nashville, TN 37203-4704 or emailed to permissions@abingdonpress.com.

Library of Congress Control Number: 2025933485

978-1-7910-3933-2

Scripture quotations unless noted otherwise are taken from the New Revised Standard Version, Updated Edition. Copyright © 2021 National Council of Churches of Christ in the United States of America. Used by permission. All rights reserved worldwide.

MANUFACTURED IN THE
UNITED STATES OF AMERICA

*For Megan, Montgomery,
Clayton, and Wade:
you are my rock and my joy!*

---

*For the members of
Woodmont Christian Church
and my students
at Vanderbilt University.*

CONTENTS

Introduction: A Wake-Up Call ix
Chapter 1: Culture 1
Chapter 2: Virtue 4
Chapter 3: Resilience 7
Chapter 4: Emotional Intelligence 12
Chapter 5: Mindset 17
Chapter 6: Overcoming Disappointment 20
Chapter 7: Happiness 24
Chapter 8: Truth 26
Chapter 9: Avoiding Contempt 29
Chapter 10: Healing 32
Chapter 11: Love 35
Chapter 12: Humility 41
Chapter 13: Peace 43
Chapter 14: Growing through Pain 48
Chapter 15: Trust 51
Chapter 16: Relationships 55
Chapter 17: Faith 58
Chapter 18: Connection 61
Chapter 19: Gratitude 64
Chapter 20: Civility 67
Chapter 21: Leadership 70
Chapter 22: Money 74
Chapter 23: Wisdom 78
Chapter 24: Priorities 81

Chapter	Title	Page
Chapter 25:	Diversity	84
Chapter 26:	Habits	88
Chapter 27:	Purpose	91
Chapter 28:	Hope	93
Chapter 29:	Simplicity	95
Chapter 30:	Sabbath	100
Conclusion:	Why Character Matters	103
Notes		107

INTRODUCTION
A Wake-Up Call

On Monday morning, March 27, 2023, I was in a meeting in my office in Nashville. Suddenly, police cars, firetrucks, and ambulances raced down Hillsboro Road. That was followed by many additional police cars, ambulances, and emergency vehicles. We would soon find out that a heavily armed shooter had walked into The Covenant School just down the street and opened fire. Six innocent people lost their lives. Three of them were nine-year-old children: Evelyn Dieckhaus, Hallie Scruggs, and William Kinney. Three adults also lost their lives: head of school Katherine Koonce, substitute teacher Cynthia Peak, and beloved custodian Mike Hill. Thanks to the heroic efforts of multiple teachers and law enforcement, many more lives were spared that day. This tragic event rocked our southern city to its very core. We were all shocked, outraged, saddened, and left in a state of utter disbelief.

I spent the afternoon at Woodmont Baptist, the church right next to ours, helping families reunite with their children. That painful process took many hours. It was hell on earth. Of course, reunification was not possible for every family. Many were called down to the hospital and received the worst news imaginable: their loved ones did not make it. It was an absolute nightmare! I have never experienced anything like that before in my life.

Introduction

Evelyn Dieckhaus was a Covenant third grader and member of our church. We held her service at our church that Friday, March 31. Evelyn was a wonderful young girl—brilliant, smart, full of hope and light. She was a blessing to her family and our church community. She had been scheduled to sing Louis Armstrong's "What a Wonderful World" at a school play. Instead, I asked my good friend Vince Gill to come and sing it at her service with his daughter on the piano. The other funerals followed in the coming days. Black-and-red ribbons remained on mailboxes and churches the rest of the year.

The grief in Nashville and across the nation was palpable. Why do we live in a world where these things happen? How does somebody get to a place where they decide to commit such an atrocity? What can we do to change it? These innocent children and teachers simply went to school and never returned home to their families, leaving a void that, for some, will never be filled.

In my life as a pastor and professor, I often ask people and groups what bothers them the most about our culture and the current state of American society. The answers always vary, but here are some of the most common responses that I hear:

- There is too much anger and hatred existing among people and groups.
- Everything has become politicized, and everybody wants to know which team you are on.
- Social media is an addiction that is out of control and is having negative effects on society. People are so obsessed with posting about their lives that

Introduction

they forget to simply live their lives. And we can't put that genie back in the bottle.

- The media drives fear and division. With a twenty-four-hour news cycle and endless commentators and channels, the media can tell you both the news and what to think about what is happening.
- People are too selfish and self-centered, thinking only about themselves and their own interests.
- Civility and respect seem to be gone. Lost are the days of disagreeing with somebody and still respecting them as fellow human beings.
- Christianity is waning in our culture, but both Christians and non-Christians have contributed to the moral rot of society. In fact, Jesus probably would not recognize the religion of many Christians today.
- Fear and anxiety are rampant and are most evident in our children.
- The growing gap between the haves and have-nots is driving crime and leading to all kinds of other problems.
- Alcohol and drug addiction seem to be ruining marriages, families, and friendships. People are addicted while trying to cope with their pain.
- Loneliness has become an epidemic.
- Character formation is simply not happening for many young people.

Introduction

How would you answer this question? What troubles you most about the times in which we are now living? What is it that keeps you up at night?

Our society seems morally adrift. This is reflected in the leaders that we choose and the way people treat one another. Truth is no longer tied to evidence and facts. Selfishness is out of control. Civility and mutual respect have been on the decline. Character formation does not happen automatically, and many people are growing up in our world without a basic understanding of what it means to be a moral person, committed to certain enduring values. Before his death in 2020, Rabbi Jonathan Sacks defined the moral life this way: "A concern for the welfare of others, an active commitment to justice and compassion, a willingness to ask not just what is good for me, but what is good for 'all of us together.'"[1] How can our culture return to emphasizing and exemplifying these values? How can we create a morally grounded culture once again?

Perhaps the most important place to start thinking about these questions is in our relationships with the people already connected to us. How we navigate these relationships is a matter of character and morality as well as a wellspring of our own happiness and satisfaction with life. A number of years ago, *Forbes* published an article on the "Top 25 Regrets" that people had in life. Their list included these things:

- working too much at the expense of family and friends,
- losing touch with good friends over time,
- not turning off the phone more often,

- not realizing that happiness is a choice,
- paying too little attention to one's marriage,
- not burying the hatchet with an old friend or family member,
- spending too little time with children,
- taking care of one's health at a young age, and
- not working to be a better mother or father.

All of these have to do with human relationships—with the love, care, sacrifice, and giving we direct toward others. How will we measure our lives when it's all said and done? How can we live our lives so that we don't have regrets at the end? Whatever the answer to this question is for us, it has to start with the quality of our relationships and how we derive meaning and joy from them.

The writer David Brooks provides a helpful metaphor. In life, we have the task of climbing two mountains. On the *first mountain* of life, we seek to establish ourselves. We leave home, go to college, get our education, we break away from our parents and become independent. We start to build a career and work toward success. This is the mountain where upward mobility is very important. We want to be respected and admired by others. We want to do things that will matter and that will be viewed as significant.

Brooks says, "On the first mountain, we all have to perform certain tasks: establish an identity, separate from our parents, cultivate our talents, build a secure ego, and try to make a mark in the world. People climbing that first mountain spend a lot of

Introduction

time thinking about reputation management. They are always keeping score. How do I measure up? Where do I rank?"[2] On the first mountain, there is a lot of time and emotion that goes into asking the questions, What do other people think about me? Am I admired and respected?

It's on the first mountain that we date and begin to look for a spouse. Choosing a spouse is one of the most important decisions we will ever make. Once we get married, we then try to start a family. Much of the first mountain is spent tending to the needs of our family. Family life is busy, it's exhausting, but it's also very rewarding. On the first mountain, there is a lot of fear: fear of failure, fear of rejection, fear of being judged, fear of not measuring up, fear of not gaining the respect and recognition that we want. Ego plays a big role on the first mountain. Ego drives us to be successful, but it also drives our disappointment when we don't achieve what we had hoped to.

Much of this first mountain mindset comes from a culture of hyper-individualism that has been prevalent now for seventy years. It started back in the 1960s with a rebellion against institutions, a desire to be free, and a concentrated focus on self, but we have now taken it too far. And in many ways, it has become a disaster. Much of our culture is all about self. Brooks says, "When a whole society is built around self-preoccupation, its members become separated from one another, divided, and alienated. This is what has happened. The rot we see in our politics is caused by a rot in our moral and cultural foundations—in the way we relate to one another."[3] We don't listen to each other. We don't treat each other well. Many people feel alienated from the

Introduction

rest of the world. They feel like nobody cares about them, and Facebook friends are not an adequate substitute.

At some point, we move ahead to the *second mountain*, which marks a major shift in how we see the world. Sometimes we choose to move to the second mountain, and sometimes something happens in life that throws us on the second mountain—cancer, a divorce, suicide of a friend or family member, an addiction, alcoholism, bankruptcy, unemployment. There are all kinds of things that can happen in life that will cause us to stop and say, "Is this all that there is? Isn't there more to life than this? Why do I feel so empty and unfulfilled?" We get sick of the rat race. Constant competition. Trying to prove who can accumulate the most money, status, and stuff. It might be fun for a while, but then it grows old.

The second mountain requires a major shift in our priorities. Brooks says, "If the first mountain is about building up the ego and defining the self, the second mountain is about shedding the ego and losing the self. If the first mountain is about acquisition, the second mountain is about contribution. If the first mountain is elitist, moving up—the second mountain is egalitarian—planting yourself amid those who need, and walking arm and arm with them."[4]

Different people arrive at the second mountain at different times. And some people never quite get there. They can spend their entire life clawing, climbing, scrapping, and seeking to conquer the first mountain. But truth be told, the first mountain doesn't really have a summit, or if you reach your own summit, you find that there are always still other people who have more

Introduction

than you—more money, more success, more status. And people who spend their entire lives on the first mountain will eventually find themselves lonely and unsatisfied.

When my wife, Megan, and I celebrated our fifteenth anniversary, we spent some time looking back over the past decade and how much things have changed: the birth of our three children, a daughter and two sons; the loss of close friends that we loved; growth in our careers; friendships that have come and gone; family dynamics that have changed. When you have a chance to contemplate your life in this way, you will often realize that commitment to others is the source of lasting meaning, satisfaction, and happiness. Because that's where relationships are formed; that's where life is truly lived. That's where joy is experienced.

I am writing this book to share some honest thoughts about what I believe our world needs now, at this particular time in history. I am writing these words as a pastor, professor, husband, and father who takes each of these roles seriously and has also garnered a bit of wisdom and perspective from each.

Life is certainly about more than what we do. It's about who we are and who we want to become over time. This is my humble attempt to talk about certain lessons and values that I believe are desperately needed in our world. In both ministry and university settings, my primary goal has been the education of character and the formation of moral leaders. Moral leadership and formation seem to be waning in our culture. Building it back up involves many aspects, including the intentional cultivation of particular virtues, spiritual formation, and psychological

Introduction

well-being. Emotional intelligence—which includes self-awareness, self-regulation, motivation, empathy, and social skills—is particularly important here.

At the most basic level, much of this has to do with developing character. Character is who you are when nobody is looking. Character is marked by the commitment to lasting values that must be taught to every generation. These values must also be modeled by the older generations in our words and actions. Nobody is perfect, but young people quickly recognize hypocrisy when they see it. I am writing from a Christian perspective, but these values are indispensable for all people, regardless of faith tradition. If we hope to build a sustainable future for our children and grandchildren, they cannot be ignored. By seeking and learning to embody them, we can improve our relationships, help reshape our culture, and find significance and meaning in our lives.

CHAPTER 1
Culture

Just before the pandemic began in early 2020, I was invited to speak to a group of attorneys in downtown Nashville. I began the talk by identifying significant challenges facing American culture at this particular time in history. Of course, two years of the coronavirus pandemic would only exacerbate all of these challenges, and they certainly remain in American society today.

First, we continue to see high levels of emptiness, meaninglessness, and rising depths of despair. Many Americans do not know their purpose and feel ignored, lost, invisible, and unloved. Depression, addiction, and suicide rates remain high.

Second, loneliness and social isolation are still on the rise. As former senator Ben Sasse says, "Among epidemiologists, psychiatrists, public health officials, and social scientists, there is a growing consensus that the number one health crisis in America right now is not cancer, not obesity, and not heart disease—it's loneliness."[1] Our culture is hyper-connected on screens and yet disconnected at the same time.

Third, extreme polarization and tribalism have led to unprecedented levels of anger and contempt, which are fueling populism and anger throughout the West. Contempt is much more dangerous than disagreement. It is the result of anger and disgust with the opposing side. Social media makes this worse.

What the World Needs Now

Fourth, there seems to be a serious shortage of healthy leaders in our culture who are grounded and well balanced. As politics has evolved into a winner-take-all blood sport, fewer and fewer normal people want to expose their family to the scrutiny and criticism that comes with being a public servant.

These are certainly not the only challenges we face, but they are real and need to be addressed. However, the ability of our society to rise to this challenge has been significantly hampered by an inability to cooperate and even discuss these issues without things devolving into a shouting match.

The day after the first Trump impeachment trial ended, Harvard professor Arthur Brooks stood before the National Prayer Breakfast in Washington, DC, in front of the president, the House speaker, senators, congressmen, diplomats, and faith leaders and boldly said the following words: "I am here today to talk about what I believe is the biggest crisis facing our nation—and many other nations—today. This is the crisis of contempt—the polarization that is tearing our society apart."[2] Brooks goes on to say that his motivation for addressing the crisis is tied directly to his Christian faith and the words of Jesus, who taught, "Love your enemies and pray for those who persecute you, so that you may be children of your Father in heaven" (Matthew 5:44-45).

Nineteenth-century philosopher Arthur Schopenhauer once defined contempt as "the unsullied conviction of the worthlessness of another."[3] Contempt ruins relationships, it ends marriages, and it has the ability to destroy our nation if we are not careful. Whether Arthur Brooks's call to action and civility

Culture

will make a difference remains to be seen. What we do know with absolute certainty is that the angry rhetoric, continual insults, and dehumanization of opponents needs to stop. What we now see in our politics is the opposite of spiritual maturity and human decency. Who has the will and the desire to turn it around? It won't be easy, and it won't happen quickly. But anybody who takes the words and example of Christ seriously needs to be part of the solution. This must include Republicans and Democrats, liberals and conservatives, Baptists and Episcopalians, the young and the old. Civil discourse, intelligent disagreement, and the exchange of competing ideas that have made this nation great for many years is being put to the ultimate test.

It is one thing to identify and name these challenges. It is another to work toward practical solutions that will create stronger communities and relationships. The ongoing evolution of the digital age allows people to interact, often in superficial or unhealthy ways, without ever having to get to truly know another person. We live in a sound-bite culture that prohibits us from seeing the nuances of complex topics. As tribalism and fear have expanded, echo chambers abound and healthy dialogue does not happen. We must remind our children that screens should not serve as the basis for relationships and getting to know other people. We all must be willing to listen to one another's stories and the many factors that cause us to feel the way we feel. But before we can begin to address these issues, we first have to name them for what they are.

CHAPTER 2
Virtue

Since at least the time of Aristotle and Socrates, virtue has been an integral part of what it means to be a well-rounded, respected, and happy person. Virtue is an established tendency to act in a certain way, which involves having a sense of how to act in a given situation to bring about a certain result. Important virtues that have been valued in many different faith and philosophical traditions and social and cultural settings include characteristics like courage, temperance, modesty, responsibility, compassion, appreciation, perseverance, honesty, and justice.

Living out any one of these virtues involves many different components and aspects of one's life. Virtuous individuals learn to think before they speak or act and recognize the clear connections between thoughts, words, and actions. How we act, what we say, the feelings we have, our thoughts and emotions are all involved when it comes to virtue. So unsurprisingly, academic and religious formation has traditionally placed a strong emphasis on the development of the entire person—mentally, physically, emotionally, and spiritually. We need to properly develop and train our whole selves to act virtuously.

Over time, however, we have seen a decline when it comes to intentionally instilling virtues in young people. Many say that virtue is written on the human heart and is thus something people can discover on their own, using their own resources.

Virtue

There is something to this idea. After all, we all have a conscience, an innate sense of right and wrong, that guides us throughout life even if we don't always take the most virtuous path. Still, it is certainly not a given that young people will discover and rightly prioritize positive virtues on their own. In fact, for most people who lack guidance, teaching, and examples to follow, a strong sense of virtue is unlikely to develop.

The development of virtue starts well before formal education; it begins in the family with parenting. Parents are called to teach their children right from wrong and good from evil and then model the way each day. Some have shied away from the concept of family values, but it's in the nuclear family unit that the seeds of virtue are first planted or not. This is extraordinarily important for a person's development and sense of self.

Many people believe that being a part of a faith tradition is not necessary for living a virtuous life, and there certainly are examples of this. And it is also true that virtue is certainly context-dependent; people will emphasize certain virtues over others and will apply their virtues in the world in different ways depending on the circumstances and their personal characteristics.

In general, though, what does it mean to be virtuous? What virtues should we aspire to? In the Christian tradition, we can look to what Paul calls the "fruit of the Spirit." He writes, "By contrast, the fruit of the Spirit is love, joy, peace, patience, kindness, generosity, faithfulness, gentleness, and self-control. There is no law against such things" (Galatians 5:22-23). I

What the World Needs Now

consider these to be the greatest of the virtues; they are simply what flows from a life that opens itself to the Spirit. These virtues are the work of God and can be seen in the example of Jesus throughout his life. And the sooner in life these attributes are impressed deeply on a person, the better the foundation that person will have for building a meaningful, fruitful, and peaceful life. Christianity does not have a monopoly on these virtues, but they are a key part of living a balanced and Spirit-filled life.

Virtuous people, both today and in centuries past, clearly understand that character is of the utmost importance, but character formation takes significant time and intentional practice. It is best begun early and practiced every single day. While this is not always easy, it is a central component of the ongoing struggle to be better and to live better, both for others and ourselves.

CHAPTER 3
Resilience

"What doesn't kill you makes you stronger." Have you heard this before? Some say this is the definition of resilience, but some might find this sentiment misguided and insensitive to people who have suffered great trauma. Perhaps there are a few steps missing between "doesn't kill you" and "makes you stronger." Certainly, our injuries can be transformed into strengths with the grace of God and the hard work of recovery and faith.

How do we define resilience and where do we find it? Why are some people able to bounce back from difficult times and others aren't? According to the American Psychological Association, *resilience* is "the process and outcome of successfully adapting to difficult or challenging life experiences, especially through mental, emotional, and behavioral flexibility and adjustment to external and internal demands."[1] Research has shown that resilience is ordinary, not extraordinary. It is not a trait that people either have or do not have. It involves behaviors, thoughts, and actions that can be learned and developed in anyone.

Resilience is similar to emotional intelligence in that it can be built and developed over time. An interesting article in the *Harvard Business Review* by Diane Coutu in 2002 says resilient people possess three defining characteristics:

What the World Needs Now

1. They accept the harsh realities that are facing them.
2. They are able to find meaning in terrible times.
3. They have an uncanny ability to improvise and make do with whatever is at hand. They are survivors.[2]

Since we will all experience pain in life, then it's also true that we should work hard to develop resilience. So how does one do that? Everybody's life is different; all of us face unique challenges and setbacks. It is hard to identify a formula for resilience. The American Psychological Association suggests several ways to build resilience.[3] I've adapted some of those ideas that I believe go a long way in helping cultivate a resilient spirit.

1. *Develop strong relationships with people.* Creating and maintaining close relationships with family members, friends, and others is important. These connections from people who truly care about you give you people to lean on for help and support during difficult times. Being active in a small group is incredibly important and should be stressed in churches. Even being there when others are in need is a way to strengthen your own resilience.
2. *In times of crisis, don't allow problems to take away your hope.* You will face tragic and stressful events. It's a part of life. While you may not be able to prevent those events from happening, you can control your response to them. Instead of giving

in to catastrophic thinking, focus on a future where life is better.

3. *Accept what you cannot change and know that change is simply a part of life.* Change is a constant that no one can avoid. Certain situations may mean that one of your goals or dreams isn't attainable. Once you accept that you can't change the circumstances through your actions, you can focus on the things that you can alter and improve.

4. *Focus on opportunities for personal growth.* Character is formed in the trials of life and through the lessons you learn. Look for ways to learn during difficult times of struggle and loss. For many people, those times can: help strengthen relationships, allow them to appreciate the things they have achieved in life, provide opportunities to forge a deeper spiritual life, and increase their overall self-esteem.

5. *Keep a broad outlook on life's challenges.* Throughout life, you will face adversity. When stressful and painful events happen, don't narrowly focus on them. Instead, view them from a broader and more long-term perspective. During the hard times, continue to try to count your blessings.

6. *Stay positive, hopeful, and optimistic.* Paul says, "Affliction produces endurance, and endurance produces character, and character produces hope, and hope does not put us to shame" (Romans 5:3-5). There is a big difference between people

who approach things positively and people who approach things negatively. At the end of the day, hope is a conscious decision that you can make regardless of what you may be going through.

7. *Self-care should be a priority.* Keeping your mind and body healthy is necessary when you are in a situation that requires resiliency. Try to maintain a healthy diet, to drink the proper amounts of water, to get regular exercise, and to get the right amount of sleep. Only you know what your body needs, so make sure that you are taking part in activities that you enjoy and that you find relaxing. Remember, self-care has never been and will never be selfish.

David Moore served as senior minister of Woodmont Christian Church from 1980 to 1987. In March 1986, his wife Dana, who was a vibrant part of the life of this church working with Christian education, lost her battle with cancer, and it understandably really did a number on David. After resigning in 1987, he left the country to do some postdoctoral work at Oxford University and wrote a short book called *The Liberating Power of Pain*. In that book he says, "The Christian faith is founded on the suffering of a single person, Jesus of Nazareth. His constant pain, brought on by rejection, misunderstanding, loneliness, and finally the crucifixion and resurrection, vividly demonstrates the whole love of God." He spells out the theological implications of Jesus's suffering, saying, "The model that we have in Jesus is that while God does not cause or desire our suffering, that very suffering can be the means by which we are caught up in an ever deeper relationship with God and with other people."[4] David wrote that because he came to believe it after experiencing it firsthand. Such wisdom about the love of God and others for us in difficult times is only truly made real to us after we experience suffering of our own.

CHAPTER 4
Emotional Intelligence

It has always been surprising to me how many people live their lives day in and day out, never thinking about the bigger picture or purpose of it all. I strongly encourage my undergraduate students to intentionally live a life that makes them unafraid to probe the deeper questions of meaning: Why are we here? What gives us purpose? Why do relationships matter? How do we define success?

Alain de Botton's book *The School of Life: An Emotional Education* lifts up the importance of emotional intelligence. "The emotionally intelligent person knows that love is a skill, not a feeling, and will require trust, vulnerability, generosity, humor, sexual understanding, and selective resignation."[1] In order to gain perspective in life, we must learn to see things from different vantage points. Emotional intelligence always involves self-awareness and self-regulation. We must become aware of how others are experiencing us. Do we listen? Are we always distracted and on our phones? Nonverbal messages matter. Emotionally intelligent individuals recognize that personal growth is always possible.

Sometimes this involves getting feedback from those we trust who know us the best. For example, I often ask my students to identify three people whom they trust and ask for three compliments (what they do well) and one area where they might improve. This type of input is incredibly valuable if we are open to becoming better human beings. Wise people always want to improve, yet far too many people lack this desire.

Lives are taken for senseless reasons. Politics are polarizing and exhausting. Tribalism is growing. Social isolation is real. As a minister, I often become overwhelmed by the amount of pain and hurt that I see. Illness, cancer, addiction, loss, divorce, grief, loneliness, racism, hatred, violence—it's all out there. When we don't deal with our own pain, we then go and hurt others, and it becomes a vicious cycle. Emotionally intelligent people learn to see above the fray. Viktor Frankl, a survivor of the Auschwitz concentration camp, wrote the classic book *Man's Search for Meaning*. One of the many insights contained in its pages is that we can survive the *how* in life as long as we know the *why*. Another is that even if we lose everything in life, there is one thing that cannot be taken away from us: our ability to choose our attitude in any given circumstance.[2]

Ecclesiastes reminds us that many of the things we pursue in search of meaning and happiness don't deliver; our efforts are futile, "vanity and a chasing after wind" (Ecclesiastes 1:14). Humans are notorious for turning to the wrong things for fulfillment and security. So much in the world is superficial. Restlessness keeps us distracted. Worry and fear keep us on edge. All great religions recognize this. Only life in God can give us meaning. Only deeper connections with others will last. As Augustine famously wrote, "Lord you have made us for yourselves, and our heart is restless until it finds its rest in you."[3]

What the World Needs Now

But how do we find rest in God when life is a constant series of ups and downs, joys and sorrows, victories and defeats, jubilations and heartbreaks? As limited human beings, we can't even begin to make sense of and comprehend it all. Centering prayer makes a difference here, as it can bring us back to a place of balance and composure. It focuses our minds on what is truly important and lasting, giving us a solid foundation on which to build a peaceful life.

When we are centered, thinking and acting in a way that is true to ourselves and faithful to God, what happens in our relationships? How does this help us live in ways that are more connected, compassionate, and loving?

In the Christian tradition, the first and best place to look for deeper insight here is Jesus's teachings. And when we study them, it is noteworthy that so many of Jesus's teachings and questions are directly tied to emotional intelligence, an idea popularized by psychologist and writer Daniel Goleman. In Goleman's understanding, emotional intelligence has five basic components: self-awareness, self-regulation, motivation, empathy, and social skills.[4] Jesus addresses each of these in various ways:

- *Self-awareness*. Jesus asks, "Why do you see the speck in your neighbor's eye but do not notice the log in your own eye? Or how can you say to your neighbor, 'Let me take the speck out of your eye'" (Matthew 7:3-4). In our culture, everybody seems to point out what's wrong with everybody else rather than doing the work of self-improvement.

Every time we point one finger at another person, we have three fingers pointing back at the primary source of most of our problems.

- *Self-regulation.* Jesus asks, "Which of you by worrying can add a single hour to your span of life?" (Matthew 6:27). Worry is essentially useless, but we worry all the time about many things, many of which will not ever occur. Worrying about the future is a sure way to ruin the present moment. We simply can't be present when we are overcome with worry.
- *Motivation.* Jesus says, "You are the salt of the earth.... You are the light of the world. A city built on a hill cannot be hid" (Matthew 5:13-14). People of faith are called to shine light in the darkness and provide healing for the brokenhearted. Many still live from day to day without motivation or a purpose.
- *Empathy.* Jesus says, "Blessed are those who mourn, for they will be comforted" (Matthew 5:4). He also says, "I was hungry and you gave me food, I was thirsty and you gave me something to drink, I was a stranger and you welcomed me, I was naked and you gave me clothing, I was sick and you took care of me, I was in prison and you visited me" (Matthew 25:35-36). Empathy involves showing compassion for those who are hurting and suffering, which includes providing the basic necessities of life.

What the World Needs Now

- *Social Skills.* The first thing Jesus did when he started his ministry was pick twelve people as his inner circle, his disciples, to be with him and share in his life and ministry. Further, his first miracle in John's Gospel was turning water into wine late into a wedding celebration. Surely, Jesus knew the importance of relationship, community, and social gatherings.

Each aspect of emotional intelligence matters greatly in spiritual development. What is remarkable about discipleship, spiritual formation, and emotional intelligence is that they can all be developed and enhanced over time. Faith and the spiritual life are ongoing processes that we never master. I tell my students that whether you are a Christian or not, you can always learn something valuable from Jesus's teachings and questions. This goes for the more practical questions about how we should treat one another and where we should devote our time and energy as well as the more complicated questions, matters of the heart, and motives. Why do we do the things that we do? What are our intentions? These are the questions that really matter and the ones that Jesus put at the forefront of his life and teaching.

CHAPTER 5

Mindset

Many people underestimate the importance of mindset and the significant role it plays in the spiritual life. Our mindset is always a choice. Viktor Frankl argues that we may not choose our circumstance, but we can always choose how to respond. I see three different types of mindsets from which we can choose.

The first is what I call the Good Friday Mindset. With this approach we are always afraid, always disappointed, disillusioned, and never satisfied. Nothing is ever good enough. Life is unfair and it never pans out the way we hope. We feel lost, we feel confused, we feel angry and let down. We blame all of our problems on other people and never take responsibility. We feel like everybody is out to get us, and we can't catch a break. The bad news keeps coming, we live afraid and anxious, and we have a hard time finding any sense of hope. It sometimes seems as though the ones who choose this mindset do not want things to get better because pessimism and complaining come naturally. This mindset is problematic, cynical, and brings other people down.

The second option is the Indifferent Mindset. We exist and go through the motions. Life is mundane, repetitive, and boring most of the time. We feel like we do the same thing over and over again. We take our loved ones for granted, and we're not truly or fully present with them. We're just kind of here, and

What the World Needs Now

that's about it. We spend a lot of time staring into our phones looking for new Instagram posts or emails to come in. Nothing really excites us. Nothing really inspires us. Sadly, many people choose to live this way.

The third mindset is the one most needed in our world right now—I call it the Easter Mindset. With the Easter Mindset, we make an intentional decision that we are sick and tired of the way things are, so we decide to live with energy, gratitude, and hope. We look at every day as a gift, and we don't take it for granted. We pay attention to sunsets, flowers, nature, and children playing. We treasure friendships, family, and spring budding all around us. We stop looking for the worst in other people and we start seeing the good. We stop focusing on what's wrong with everybody else and we start asking where we can improve and help others. A key component to cultivating the Easter Mindset is recognizing that there is a multibillion-dollar industry out there that exists to keep us afraid all the time. We call it "the news." And in this business, it has become increasingly difficult to differentiate between what is true and what isn't, what is fact and what is opinion, what is relevant and what is noise.

When we live our lives afraid all the time, scared all the time, we tune into this media machine and we can't seem to turn it off. It becomes addicting and consuming. I believe with all my heart that is not the way Jesus wants us to live life. Two of his consistent messages throughout the Gospels are "do not worry" and "do not be afraid" (Matthew 6:25-34; 10:31). Excessive fear squanders our life, reducing its quality and affecting others as

Mindset

well. It can even lead to emotional paralysis. Once we cultivate this Easter Mindset, we quickly recognize that fear does not win, love wins. Death does not win, life wins. The evil of this world does not win. God wins over and over again. Once we learn to live this way, we will see the world differently and discover meaning, joy, and fullness of life.

CHAPTER 6

Overcoming Disappointment

Rabbi Harold Kushner wrote a powerful book titled *Overcoming Life's Disappointments*. The book is based on the story of Moses, a pivotal figure in the Hebrew Bible. We can learn a great deal from Moses's life and the many disappointments he had to face when leading the Israelites through the wilderness. He persevered and pressed forward despite continual setbacks, inconveniences, and frustrations. He faced pursuing armies, hunger, harsh conditions, his people turning on him, and much more. To be sure, Moses did question his suitability for this job, and he got angry and sometimes made rash decisions with far-reaching consequences. But his ultimate commitment to God and the survival of his people (who were most often the source of his disappointment) did not waver. He weathered these disappointments with faithful assurance and steadfastness.

So, Kushner asks, "What if we could be like Moses in our ability to overcome disappointments, frustrations, and the denial of our dreams? What if we could learn from Moses how to respond to disappointment with faith in ourselves and in our future and to respond to heartbreak with wisdom instead of bitterness and depression?"[1]

Many of the disappointments that we face in life seem to fall into three basic categories. The first has to do with our relationships. We often learn at an early age that people will let us down. We want to become friends with somebody but discover they don't have time for us. Marriages don't work out, and people who never considered divorce go through that very painful, life-altering process. Some who go into marriage thinking everything will be perfect become disillusioned when they discover that no marriage is perfect.

The second type of disappointment revolves around work, money, and success. Some feel they should be further along their career path than they are and that they deserve to make more money than they do. Some are unfulfilled in their jobs, going through the motions every day to make a living while looking around and seeing that everybody else seems to have a better life. Social media has led us into a dangerous age of constant and easy comparison that often leads to envy and resentment. This can lead to lasting feelings of inadequacy and inferiority.

The third area of disappointment revolves around our health. We see pictures of ourselves when we were younger and thinner and wonder, *What happened?* Our bodies start to ache and give out on us, and we get frustrated. We can't do the things we used to do. We face medical challenges—some that we can control (or try to) but many that we can't. Many become frustrated that they can't live the way they used to and do all the things they once could.

The human condition involves confronting and living through the reality of such disappointments. They are inevitable. Some will experience more disappointment than others, but we all experience it on a regular basis.

What the World Needs Now

The key question is how we can overcome it. Managing expectations is very important. In marriage and relationships especially but also in jobs and even on vacations, we sometimes expect too much, putting too much pressure on things to be all that we dreamed of. Having standards is one thing, but that can sometimes, even without our being aware of it, tend toward perfectionism and unrealistic expectations.

Also, gratitude—making sure to consistently count our blessings—is essential. It is important to allow yourself to feel disappointment and the emotions that come with it. But this can't be the end of the matter. For many people, a daily practice of gratitude can be transformative. It allows us to focus on the many gifts and joys we are given in this life, both big picture and in the smallest of moments, and not simply ruminate on the negative. This can be done through prayer, silent meditation, or sharing out loud with another person.

Mindset and its effect on resilience always matter. Disappointment can serve as motivation for us to press ahead and try again. In many instances, we can reframe disappointment as an opening for something better to come along, for a change that we can shape for the better. Far too many people become disappointed for whatever reason and then never try again. Our answer should be to not let disappointment have the final say in our lives.

Kushner's challenge is for us to look to figures like Moses, who did just this. We don't know precisely what Moses was thinking and how he managed to cope after facing one disappointment after another for so many years. Even at the end of his life, after forty years in the wilderness leading his people, he did not get to witness Israel enter the Promised Land. And he knew that his people were sure to falter after he died. But at the same time, he knew that God would never entirely desert them; that with God, there is always hope for a better future.

CHAPTER 7
Happiness

A recent Pew Research report found that the number of American adults who self-identify as Christians is down 12 percent just in the past decade. In that same time period, the number of religiously unaffiliated adults in the United States grew by 30 million people.

What is happening here? No doubt, some of this is a reaction to "bad religion" that has done emotional damage and harm in the lives of many. (Accusing religious people of being hypocrites is not a new phenomenon; Jesus did it often.) Some is just a result of large-scale cultural trends, the same trends that lead people to belong to fewer civic organizations and organized social groups and have less trust in institutions.

What I find interesting is that increases in this number of religiously unaffiliated people coincide with growing levels of depression, loneliness, and meaninglessness. Many simply do not know where to turn for meaning and connection and feel as though they live alone on a deserted island. This is not an argument that religion is the only way to find meaning. I am simply pointing out that as many have turned away from religion, the void has not been filled. Or if it has been filled, it has not been filled with an adequate substitute. So it is not surprising to me that as religious commitment has declined, unhappiness and emptiness have gone up.

Many who turn away from religion are rejecting a notion or concept of God that simply doesn't make sense in their minds.

What has perhaps not occurred to a good number of these individuals is the idea of replacing that understanding with a different one, a healthier one that perhaps better reflects what we find in the Bible and the broader Christian tradition.

Union Seminary president Serene Jones puts it this way in her memoir *Call It Grace*: "If by God you mean an entity that hovers somewhere above us, watching all we do and constantly judging if we are doing right or wrong, then no.... But if you mean believing that the universe is ultimately loved by a divine reality that is greater and more wonderful than we can begin to imagine, and that in this reality we find our ultimate destiny, the purpose of our existence, then yes."[1] This all-loving God is much closer to the God of Jesus than the caricature of a white-bearded, vengeful, and exacting king on a throne that some segments of our culture envision. This latter understanding is a false god, a god that is hard to sustain faith in, especially when life gets difficult and we realize we can't help making mistakes.

All of life is theological, and there is certainly a lot of bad theology out there. We must guard against accepting the poor substitutes that our culture (sometimes parts of our own Christian culture) tries to play off as God. This is especially important because we are particularly susceptible to such deceptions. Human beings will believe in a god in their own making if they cannot find God in their lives. The desire for God, I believe, is imprinted on our soul; it is as innate and natural as our desire for happiness. And, lucky for us, these two most foundational drives support each other, help each other along, propelling us both toward God and a happier and more fulfilling life.

CHAPTER 8

Truth

What has become exceptionally clear to me in the aftermath of each major election in the past several years is not just that we have both sore winners and losers, that the pollsters are struggling to understand what's happening, or that neither side can claim to speak for the whole country. Rather, it is becoming more and more evident to me that we continue to live in a time when intelligent people simply cannot agree on what the truth is. Facts seem to be evasive, debatable, and difficult to find. As Daniel Patrick Moynihan once said, "You are entitled to your own opinion, but you are not entitled to your own facts."[1] It now feels like we live in a culture in which different groups have their own sets of facts.

When I first entered Princeton Seminary over twenty-two years ago, we talked about the many challenges of doing ministry in a "postmodern" age. Nobody really knew exactly what that meant, and a lot of different ideas were thrown around. In general, however, postmodernity is the idea that reality is no longer grounded in rationality but in individual experience. In postmodernity, realities are subject to change and can be viewed as social constructs that limit individuals. It is grounded in a skepticism and even a rejection of the grand ideologies and narratives that defined the modern era. In other words, you cannot tell others what their lived reality is because, by definition, it is theirs. So here we are, almost two decades later, and it's all making sense. If the truth is relative, then it's always up for grabs. The recurring problem with postmodernity is that it leads to constant chaos and uncertainty.

What continues to concern me is that we live in an age that often does not seem tethered by evidence. If there is clear evidence of widespread voter fraud in an election, it needs to be brought forward, for example. We have independent courts for that reason. On a macro level, the postmodern mindset is problematic because we do not have a shared set of facts, and frankly, the situation has become utterly exhausting. And it leads to a continual erosion of trust—trust in institutions, like government, churches, nonprofits, and civic groups, and in people, both neighbors and strangers, both our perceived enemies and those who agree with us.

Many no longer know where to find accurate information that is not biased or slanted by one agenda or another. Still, seeking the truth is undoubtedly worth it. It is part and parcel of living a moral life. Thinkers of many times, cultures, and ages have recognized the value of truly trying to discern the truth. Ralph Waldo Emerson once said, "truth is the property of no individual, but is the treasure of all men."[2] Henry David Thoreau said, "Rather than love, than money, than fame, give me truth."[3] And as Jesus taught, "You will know the truth, and the truth will make you free" (John 8:32). We must continue to look for, discern, and try to find truth because it does ultimately matter and it will set us free.

What the World Needs Now

But one of the greatest challenges in our culture today is that many do not know where to go to find truth. We see two news stations talking about the exact same story with completely different facts. What are we to make of this? In the world of social media, we don't know what to believe online. What is free speech and what is just half-truths and lies? What has been filtered or edited? At the end of the day, we must look at different sources and do our best to draw our own considered conclusions about what we believe to be true. At the same time, we must listen to others and hear what they believe. Truth will indeed set us free, but only after we have worked hard to discern and find it.

CHAPTER 9
Avoiding Contempt

Perhaps the greatest spiritual challenge facing American culture at this moment in history is contempt. Harvard professor Arthur C. Brooks has been writing extensively on this subject and puts it this way in his book *Love Your Enemies*: "Believing your foe is motivated by hate leads to something far worse: contempt. While anger seeks to bring someone back into the fold, contempt seeks to exile. It attempts to mock, shame, and permanently exclude from relationships by belittling, humiliating, and ignoring. While anger says, 'I care about this,' contempt says, 'You disgust me and are beneath caring about.'"[1] Contempt becomes toxic in relationships, marriages, businesses, families, and communities.

How did we get to this place? Civility and decency did not just disappear overnight. One reason is that as a society, we have lost our moral and spiritual center. Self-centeredness abounds. We have lost respect for our common humanity. Also, we have elected leaders who fan the flames of anger and contempt, which causes us to think it is acceptable to behave in similar ways. Political and ideological divides are not new; what is new is our inability to rationally discuss competing ideas in a civil manner.

What the World Needs Now

Rabbi Jonathan Sacks articulates it this way in his incredible book *Morality*: "Something new is happening: the sense that the other side is less than fully human, that its supporters are not part of the same moral community as us, that somehow their sensibilities are alien and threatening, as if they were not the opposition in a political arena, but the enemy full stop."[2] Sacks talks about multiple complex factors that have played a role: deepening Western individualism, the expansion of the internet, toxic social media, and the seemingly ever-expanding gap between the haves and the have-nots.

So what's the solution? How can we avoid having feelings of contempt for others who may have wildly different views from ours? That's the complicated part because we are all complicit and we have all played some role in getting to this point. Four important words come to mind. First, *community*. The pandemic fractured and isolated our communities in ways never seen. We need to be around one another more in real time and space and not just on a screen. Second, *friendship*. We must be intentional about becoming friends with people who see and experience things differently. Every person's life experience is unique, we all have our own lenses and backgrounds, and we simply cannot dictate to others how they should understand the world and their place in it. Third, *morality*. Part of living a moral life is listening to others and treating them with dignity and respect. Being religious is not a prerequisite to being moral. Last, *forgiveness*. Our cancel-happy culture has lost sight of what it means to practice forgiveness. We are all flawed and imperfect creatures. We all say and do things that we regret. But our inability to forgive one another has become a major problem, and judging people by their worst moments or actions is simply unfair and unjust. On the contrary, we should all strive to see the good in one another in spite of our faults, failures, and differences.

CHAPTER 10

Healing

In this age of moral outrage, polarization, and contempt, how can we strive to live a life of humility that seeks to heal deep pain and division? How can we heed Micah's timeless directive to "do justice and to love kindness and to walk humbly with your God" (Micah 6:8)? How can we keep from developing an overly exalted opinion of ourselves in a culture marked by argument, protest, rugged individualism, and self-righteousness?

Tony Jarvis, the former headmaster at Roxbury Latin, a storied prep school in Boston, once gave a powerful homily in which he identified three meaningful phrases we should all say more often.

First, he says, we should never be afraid to say, "I'm wrong." Oh, how we hate to say those words. We feel humiliated, ashamed, embarrassed, weak, and vulnerable. Jarvis says, "How hard it is to say, 'I was wrong.' How tempting it is to make artful excuses, to pass the buck to someone else or to some force beyond our control. How tempting it is to lie, and obfuscate, and evade. How terribly hard it is to face up and say, 'I'm wrong.'"[1] But being able to admit when we are wrong in life is one of the most important things that we can ever do. In 2010, Kathryn Schulz published the book *Being Wrong*, which delves into the widespread human discomfort with a kind of experience that all human beings share. Drew Faust, former president of Harvard

University, claims that it's the one book she would recommend to her students. Schulz says, "To err is to wander, and wandering is the way we discover the world; and, lost in thought, it is also the way we discover ourselves. Being right might be gratifying, but in the end it is static, a mere statement. Being wrong is hard and humbling, and sometimes even dangerous, but in the end it is a journey, and a story."[2] Too many people in this culture think they are never wrong. But how will we ever learn anything in life if we are always right? Being able to admit mistakes and errors and live with them is often the first step toward learning and transformation.

Second, according to Jarvis, we should learn to say, "I'm sorry." Saying "I'm sorry" shows strength, and not weakness. We all make mistakes. We all overreact. We all treat people badly from time to time. We all do and say things that we regret. Healthy relationships are impossible if we are not willing to apologize. In fact, in our relationships, vulnerability and trust go hand in hand. That is, closeness, love, and trust mean learning to say "I'm sorry" more often and truly mean it. Marriages could be stronger if we would apologize more often. Business relationships could be better. Friendships could be closer. Learning to apologize and apologize well are key skills that, in spite of our initial hesitancy, can grant us something profound.

Third, we should all learn to say "thank you" more often, speaking those words to friends, family, neighbors, strangers, and God. If the COVID-19 pandemic taught us anything, it's how many basic things in life we take for granted—gatherings,

What the World Needs Now

connections, celebrations, embraces. Jarvis tells us, "It is my experience that the happy people are those who assume nothing and who live each day aware of their good fortune—giving thanks for all they do enjoy, however little that may be."[3] Quite often, the happiest people in life are those who take the time to count their blessings, especially in difficult times.

CHAPTER 11

Love

The Most Reverend Michael Curry, presiding bishop of the Episcopal Church, published a timely book in 2020 called *Love Is the Way: Holding on to Hope in Troubling Times*. It is hard to argue that we do live in troubled times. Curry rose to fame in 2018 when he was asked to preside over the royal wedding of Prince Harry and Meghan Markle in London at Westminster Abbey. On that day, billions watched from around the world, and Curry discovered that his core message resonated across the globe, in every nation, with all people. As he writes in his book, "Beyond our national identities and loyalties, beyond our political sympathies and ideologies, beyond our religious and spiritual convictions and commitments, there is a universal hunger at the heart of every human being: to love and to be loved."[1] It is upon this universal desire that Christianity is based.

When he was asked by a lawyer which teaching in the law is the greatest, Jesus responded, "'You shall love the Lord your God with all your heart and with all your soul and with all your mind.' This is the greatest and first commandment. And a second is like it: 'You shall love your neighbor as yourself'" (Matthew 22:37-39). Jesus came to teach *agape*, a sacrificial love that seeks the good and well-being of others, of society, and the world. It has been described as unconquerable goodwill toward other people. Agape love is what often seems to be missing in our broken world.

What the World Needs Now

We look around and see raging polarization, economic strife, hostility, resentment, and what often feels like chaos. We see anger, fear, and many who live depressed and hopeless, unsure about the future or whether anybody cares. Many who do not love were never loved themselves, thus perpetuating the cycle. But the opposite of love has never been hate. Rather, the opposite of love is selfishness often grounded in fear. If love focuses outwardly on others, selfishness focuses inwardly. According to Curry, "Selfishness is the most destructive force in all the cosmos, and hate is only its symptom. Selfishness destroys families. Selfishness destroys communities. Selfishness has destroyed societies, nations, and global communities, and it will destroy the human race by laying waste to our planet. If we let it."[2]

The good news is that we don't have to let this be the case. We can choose love. We can choose compassion. We can choose sympathy and benevolence. Romantic love is great, but it often fades and must give way to a deeper partnership. Couples who have been married for decades have learned to honor their friendship and companionship while avoiding contempt. What our world and country need now is more agape love, where we begin to look beyond self to the needs and hurts of others. Curry says, "Where selfishness excludes, love makes room and includes. Where selfishness puts down, love lifts up. Where selfishness hurts and harms, love helps and heals. Where selfishness enslaves, love sets free and liberates."[3] Every day, we have a choice to make. Will we live to love others, or will

Love

we live for self? When we are stressed, tired, and in the wilderness of life, it may seem difficult. But choosing to love is always the right move.

Human beings are complicated creatures. God has created us in God's own image, and God has given us the capacity to love others, to care for others, to help others. Thank goodness we don't have to go through life alone. We live in community. We believe in community. We journey through life together, supporting one another. But there is another side to us as well. And it's this side that we're not all that proud of. Sometimes, it seems like love gets pushed aside, and anger, resentment, selfishness, jealousy, bitterness, and hostility can take over. And this isn't the way we want to be; it's just the way that we sometimes get when things happen and certain circumstances arise in life. All of us, no matter who we are, live with the ongoing tension of this struggle between the way God wants us to be and the way that our sinful nature often causes us to be. We all wrestle with this because we're all capable of both extremes.

If you had to sum up the essence of the Christian faith in one word, *love* would be a good one. In fact, I think it would be the best choice. Some of the Pharisees ask Jesus, "Teacher, which commandment in the law is the greatest?" And he responds, saying, "'You shall love the Lord your God with all your heart and with all your soul and with all your mind.' This is the greatest and first commandment. And a second is like it: 'You shall love your neighbor as yourself'" (Matthew 22:36-39). This is Jesus's most central commandment to us, his summation of the law and the gospel.

What the World Needs Now

Jesus reiterates the importance of love throughout his teaching: "I give you a new commandment, that you love one another...as I have loved you" (John 13:34). "You have heard that it was said, 'You shall love your neighbor and hate your enemy.' But I say to you: Love your enemies and pray for those who persecute you" (Matthew 5:43-44). "In everything do to others as you would have them do to you" (Matthew 7:12).

Then we find the beautiful and timeless words of the apostle Paul in his letter to the Corinthians. We know these words. They are read at weddings all the time. We are familiar with them, yet do we read them slowly enough to really listen to what they are saying? Do we take in the message deeply and allow it to settle over our whole being? "Love is patient; love is kind; love is not envious or boastful or arrogant or rude. It does not insist on its own way; it is not irritable; it keeps no record of wrongs; it does not rejoice in wrongdoing but rejoices in the truth. It bears all things, believes all things, hopes all things, and endures all things. Love never ends" (1 Corinthians 13:4-8).

As human beings, we're pretty good at falling in love. We're pretty good at loving those who are kind to us, loving those whom we are closest to. But that's not the love that Jesus came to teach. That's not necessarily the kind of love that Paul is talking about in 1 Corinthians—even though it's perfectly fitting and normal to read this passage at weddings.

As noted above, Jesus came to teach us agape. And agape love is a very mature, advanced form of love. Most human beings simply don't get it—at least not at first. Maybe they don't want to get it. Maybe it's too hard. Maybe it seems unreasonable.

Love

Agape love means learning to love everybody because God already loves everybody. Agape love means learning to love in the face of hurt, love in the face of betrayal, love in the face of hate. We will spend our entire lives trying to grasp the totality of what agape love is all about. It is an ideal for us, one of the goals of life that we may never quite attain but remains an ongoing task to more fully realize.

There are powerful words in the First Epistle of John: "Beloved, let us love one another, because love is from God; everyone who loves is born of God and knows God. Whoever does not love does not know God, for God is love.... There is no fear in love, but perfect love casts out fear; for fear has to do with punishment, and whoever fears has not reached perfection in love" (4:7-8, 18). We tend to think of hate as being the opposite of love. But if you stop and think of some of the reasons why people don't love—they've been hurt before, they don't want to be hurt again, they don't know the other person, they're scared of being rejected and not receiving the same love in return—these all have to do with fear. And the passage above from 1 John is clear that perfect love casts out fear. If we're honest, it's usually fear that keeps us from loving. And since we live in a world that seems to be full of fear, I think it's obvious that we need more love.

If you talk to couples who have been married for many years or to people who have been able to maintain lifelong friendships, and ask them the secret to their relationships, they will probably tell you that they have learned to be committed to each other no matter what may happen. They have learned to bear

What the World Needs Now

each other's burdens, to forgive each other, and to see the bigger picture in life.

Long-lasting love can bear any insult, any injury, and any disappointment. Long-lasting love realizes that life is a journey full of ups and downs, full of joys and sorrows, full of good times as well as bad times, full of hopes and disappointments. But if we learn to see the bigger picture in life, then we come to understand that life is a marathon and not a sprint. And even though there are times in all of our relationships when we grow weary and frustrated and get worn out, in the end, commitment, forgiveness, and perseverance are the keys to lifelong love.

If you can master your temper, then you can master just about anything in life. All of us have our boiling points—some get there faster than others. All of us can get pushed to the point that if we don't learn to walk away, to get our distance, to let things go, then we risk losing the capacity to love, because we have so much anger built up and we can do great damage to relationships, friendships, marriages—damage that can never be repaired.

Love is not easy. Love is not simple. Jesus knew this. Paul knew this. So we should acknowledge this too. Love requires commitment and hard work. But it has also been and always will be the force that holds everything together in this world. So may we never forget that. And may we always remember that God has put us here to love one another—even when it's hard. And God expects us to love one another—even when it's hard.

CHAPTER 12
Humility

Humility is a virtue that doesn't get enough attention in our culture. With the rapid rise of social media, we seem to reward self-promotion, self-aggrandizement, and alarming levels of narcissism. Humble people often get overlooked. But why? Humility is actually a sign of great strength. It is an attribute that we should want to teach our children. However, this is getting much more challenging in a society that so often rewards self-promotion. But we know that all human beings have character flaws and blind spots. Coming to terms with ours will not only keep us humble but also help us grow into more well-rounded and conscientious people.

David Brooks says this about humility: "In the struggle against your own weakness, humility is the greatest virtue. Humility is having an accurate assessment of your own nature and your own place in the cosmos."[1] Too many people in our culture think that they are the center of the universe, and everything revolves around them. With this mindset, they will wait for others to cater to their every need. Humble people do not bring all conversations back to themselves. They show genuine interest in the lives and needs of others. They ask thought-provoking questions to those around them. In short, they are not preoccupied with their own self. Humble people do not always have to get credit for successes, and they

What the World Needs Now

are willing to empower others and lift them up. They are also willing to own their own mistakes and failures rather than cast blame on others. This is an especially important skill for leaders to develop in order to build trust and create an atmosphere of care and safety.

Pride, the opposite of humility, is a very complicated topic. It can quickly lead to arrogance and a sense of superiority. Jesus echoed this sentiment in the Gospels when he said, "All who exalt themselves will be humbled, but all who humble themselves will be exalted" (Luke 18:14). Maintaining humility keeps us grounded in life. We all have a vice or core sin that is deeply intertwined with our personality. Think of the seven deadly ones: pride, greed, wrath, envy, lust, gluttony, and sloth. These challenges are real, legitimate, and continuous. The thought patterns and behaviors associated with these negative characteristics greatly affect our relationships and interactions with others. But they do not need to define us. These are simply obstacles on the human journey that we must work to overcome.

Thomas Keating once said, "We are kept from the experience of the Spirit because our inner world is cluttered with past traumas.... As we begin to clear away this clutter, the energy of divine light and love begins to flow through our being."[2] Humility is part of this clearing away. It allows us to grow and become at peace with our shortcomings, recognize areas for improvement, and foster solid, peaceful relationships with those around us.

CHAPTER 13

Peace

What does it mean to be a peaceful person? I've given lots of thought to this question over the years—not because I have perfected it in any way but because I try to constantly strive for it. I think it is immensely important. Healthy people do their very best to live peaceably with others.

In order to begin thinking about and creating peace, it may be helpful to understand some of the common occurrences that tend to lead to conflict in our lives:

- *Not being heard.* There is nothing worse than feeling as though your voice doesn't matter. So we should do our very best to listen to others and to hear them out—not to fix their problems but to hear them.
- *Feeling disrespected.* When we feel disrespected for whatever reason, it leaves us in a bad place. It makes us angry and resentful, disrupting our inner peace.
- *Experiencing envy.* When somebody is envious of another person and what they have, it's hard for that person to find peace. It's hard for them to be thankful. Somebody in my church once told me that envy is the worst of all the deadly sins because we don't even enjoy it for a little while.
- *Being full of fear.* Those who live their lives in fear rarely find inner peace because they are always

worried about what is going to happen. But the Bible tells us that "perfect love casts out fear" (1 John 4:18).

In order to counter these disruptors of peace, we should seek to cultivate ways of thinking and acting that can help overcome them. Here are five habits of peaceful people:

1. *To be a peaceful person, we first understand the transforming power of forgiveness.* Every single one of us has been done wrong by somebody. Somebody has hurt us. Somebody has offended, disrespected, or ignored us. As human beings, we all have that in common. And Jesus taught us to forgive because refusing to forgive allows negativity and hurt to linger in our hearts. Forgiveness doesn't mean you forget, but it does mean that you let it go. Forgiveness doesn't mean that you set yourself up to be hurt again, but it does mean that you have to leave the hurt in the past and move on. Forgiveness is not always easy, but it is necessary if you want to live a peaceful life.

2. *To be a peaceful person, we must realize we can't control everything and so we shouldn't try to.* Stanley Hauerwas, in his book *The Peaceable Kingdom*, says: "Our need to be in control is the basis for the violence of our lives. For since our 'control' and 'power' cannot help but be built on an insufficient basis, we must use force to maintain

the illusion that we are in control. We are deeply afraid of losing what unity of self we have achieved. Any idea or person threatening that unity must either be manipulated or eliminated."[1] There are many more things that we cannot control, most centrally other people, what they do, and how they think. But there are some things in life that we can control. Despite what it sometimes seems like, our level of inner peace is one of these things. Developing the ability to distinguish between what can and can't be controlled is one of the key steps in creating inner peace.

3. *To be a peaceful person, we cannot get sucked into unnecessary conflict with non-peaceful people.* It has always taken two to fight. If somebody is combative, manipulative, or passive-aggressive and you get tangled up with them, there is sometimes just no way to win since you just get sucked into an endless series of conflicts. Many times, avoidance is a better option, if possible. That's why Jesus said turn the other cheek, go the extra mile. This is simply a way of illustrating the power of refusing to get drawn into a fight. Sometimes silence is the best response for building up peace.

4. *Being a peaceful person means learning what it means to be fully present in the moment.* Don't live in the past; don't obsess about the future. Somebody once asked a Zen master what monks

do, and he responded, "We eat, we sleep, we walk." The person then replied, "Well I too eat, sleep, and walk, and I'm not a monk." The Zen master replied, "Yes, but when I eat, I know I am eating. When I sleep, I know I am sleeping. When I walk, I know I am walking." We have all mastered the challenge of multitasking with the help of technology. We pride ourselves on it. But in the process, we have forgotten what it means to be fully present. We are distracted. Our minds are somewhere else. Peaceful people, however, know what it means to be fully present in the moment.

5. *Perhaps most important, being a peaceful person means that we find peace with ourselves.* Those who are the most combative, most angry, most aggressive, are almost always those who are not at peace with themselves, and so they take it out on everybody else. That's why Jesus always focused on the heart—inner peace naturally leads to peace with others.

But how do you make peace with yourself? It starts with addressing our own hurt and pain. Being at peace with ourselves is something we will spend our entire lives trying to do. But it is impossible to be a peaceful person if you are always at war in your own heart. The truth is, we all play a major part in shaping the type of world this is going to be. And it starts in our hearts and spreads outward from there.

Peace

    Jesus, always concerned with matters of the heart, knew this well. Before he left his disciples, Jesus said: "Peace I leave with you; my peace I give to you. I do not give to you as the world gives. Do not let your hearts be troubled, and do not let them be afraid" (John 14:27). Are we listening? The way of Jesus will always be the way of peace.

CHAPTER 14

Growing through Pain

The most difficult part of any minister's job is helping people work through their pain. Divorce, addiction, depression, loneliness, infidelity, financial hardship, fear, worry, and relentless anxiety are all real problems in our complicated world. Thich Nhat Hanh, in *The Art of Living*, says, "Many of us want to do something to help the world suffer less. We see so much violence, poverty, and environmental destruction all around us. But if we are not peaceful, if we don't have enough compassion, then we can't do much to help. We ourselves are the center. We have to make peace and reduce the suffering in ourselves first, because we represent the world. Peace, compassion, and well-being begin with ourselves."[1] This is a truth that many overlook.

Jesus commands us to love others as we love ourselves, but I am convinced that many people are doing the opposite of that: they are hurting others because they themselves are hurting inside. It is a vicious and dangerous cycle. It's only when we first tend to our own soul and healing that we can then tend to others. Most of the time when people lash out in anger, there is something going on inside. But the question still remains: How do we grow through our pain? How does it change us? How does it make us stronger? Sometimes the pain is so great that we can lose our perspective, lose our hope.

Growing through Pain

Jerry Sittser is a pastoral theology professor at Whitworth University. Years ago, he lost his wife, daughter, and mother in a car accident that he and his other children survived. He wrote an incredible book after that experience titled *A Grace Disguised: How the Soul Grows through Loss,* and I have given it to many people over the years. It is, perhaps, the best book I have ever read on loss and grief. Sittser says, "The soul is elastic, like a balloon. It can grow larger through suffering. Loss can enlarge its capacity for anger, depression, despair, and anguish—all natural and legitimate emotions whenever we experience loss. But once enlarged, the soul is also capable of experiencing greater joy, strength, peace, and love." He says, "Those who suffer loss live suspended between a past for which they long and a future for which they hope. Catastrophic loss by definition precludes recovery. It will transform us or destroy us, but it will never leave us the same. There is no going back to the past which is gone forever, only going ahead to the future which is yet to be discovered."[2] Life is certainly full of hurts and pains, but all of us should try and make the decision, whenever possible, to grow through it.

In over twenty years of ordained ministry, I have had the unique opportunity to help countless people through some very difficult situations: loss of a child, divorces, miscarriages, terminal illnesses, school shootings, unemployment, severe addictions, depression, and much more. What I have discovered is that every challenge we face in life can ultimately strengthen us in the big picture. That doesn't mean it is easy to go through any situation or that we should want to go through hard times.

49

What the World Needs Now

It just means that once we make it through, we are able to become tougher, stronger, and more resilient than before. We should not live with the illusion that life is always going to be easy. That is simply not reality. We all struggle and experience pain. However, everything that we go through can prepare us for future situations and for helping others. Often, the best compassion and pastoral care we can muster are the direct result of our own pain, helping others get through challenges we have already faced.

CHAPTER 15

Trust

When historians look back on the late twentieth and early twenty-first centuries, this period will be marked as a time of declining trust in American institutions. This has been true in government, medicine, higher education, business, technology, and religion. An article published in *The Wall Street Journal*, "How American Institutions Went from Trust to Bust," specifically names some of the historical events that have led to this diminished trust. These include:

- The claim of weapons of mass destruction in 2003 that led to invading Iraq. The weapons never materialized.
- Bankers in 2008 who said the financial system was sound.
- Technology companies that told users that their personal data was secure only later to have these data breached.
- Big businesses that turned to extreme woke ideology.
- Lawmakers of both parties who have said they are controlling illegal immigration only to have massive amounts of illegal immigrants streaming across the border.

What the World Needs Now

- Claims of Russian interference in the 2016 election.
- Claims of a stolen election in 2020.
- Health officials telling everybody to follow the science, but the science seemed to change with politics.[1]

All of these have played a role in getting us to where we are today. Combined with social media and bitter partisanship, it has been a challenging stretch for American society.

It is not just institutions that have suffered because of this; individuals are now much less likely to trust each other. The article states, "The rapid loss of confidence is startling and unprecedented. It has ominous implications for the cohesion, prosperity, and even survival of the US. Trust is the essential feature that allows a society to function—more important the more modern and complex society grows."[2] Simply put, we are all suffering from this deficit of trust in our culture. And the church has not been immune to this: with sex scandals, political infighting, and overt partisanship, many have turned away from organized religion, even while still maintaining a strong personal faith and spirituality.

There are several ways that everyone can help rebuild trust in our society:

- *Seek to always tell the truth.* That sounds obvious, but people often shy away from the truth because it is uncomfortable. Jesus tells us, "You will know the truth, and the truth will make you free" (John 8:32). When you tell the truth, you don't have to remember what you said and keep track of what is real versus embellished or simply fabricated. Unfortunately, we seem to be living in an age where basic facts are disputed. It used to be that we were entitled to our own opinions. Now it seems like many people simply come up with their own facts.

- *Become friends with people who have different politics and ideologies.* In the age of social media, homogenous echo chambers have become a big problem. If we are only around people who agree with us, how will we ever be challenged? How will we ever grow and expand our worldview?
- *Seek the goodness in people.* So often, we look for what is wrong or what we don't like. However, we all have good in us because we are all children of God. Let's learn to focus more on what brings us together rather than what divides. At the end of the day, we have far more in common with one another, but we always seem to focus on differences.
- *Let others know when they have betrayed your trust.* What often happens is somebody betrays our trust, and we just write them off. What if we took the time to say, "This was very hurtful, and it will be difficult for me to trust you again." This doesn't prescribe a certain outcome, but it does open the door for healing, honesty, and renewal.

What the World Needs Now

Trust is the currency of healthy relationships. It matters greatly in our culture. We must work to build it and sustain it. Without trust, relationships will always suffer. One of the greatest compliments we can pay another person is to tell them that we trust them.

CHAPTER 16

Relationships

In American culture, we often define ourselves by our profession: lawyer, doctor, electrician, minister, teacher, therapist. That is often one of the first questions we ask when meeting someone new: what do you do? As if that tells us the whole story about someone. Perhaps we need to put just as much of an emphasis on the other roles we play in life, the ones that are likely more central to our identities as well as our happiness and fulfillment: husband, wife, father, mother, sister, brother, son, daughter. These are the roles that matter most in the big picture.

Relationships matter immensely in life, perhaps more than anything else, but they are also undoubtedly complicated. They are our source of great joy, happiness, and fulfillment as well as great pain, heartache, and disappointment. Everybody inevitably experiences both sides at one time or another.

My family and I once took a trip to Virginia, where we celebrated the fiftieth wedding anniversary of my wife's parents. They were college sweethearts at DePauw University and got married after graduation at age twenty-two back in 1968. It was a joy to celebrate with them and to see how their love has grown and deepened over the years. Unfortunately, fifty-year wedding anniversaries are not as common as they used to be. People today are getting married later in life, and as of 2024, the United States

What the World Needs Now

divorce rate remains around 40 percent for first marriages and is higher for subsequent ones.[1]

John Gottman, the celebrated psychologist and marriage researcher, claims that the key determining question to ask when assessing whether a marriage will last or not boils down to this: does the couple learn to honor and respect their friendship? This is much more challenging than it sounds. It certainly isn't automatic. We have to work hard to avoid criticism, defensiveness, contempt, and stonewalling, all of which lead to further and larger problems if left unchecked. Contempt can become toxic over time, infecting the whole relationship; it is a clear sign that a relationship needs work and maybe some outside help to get back on track.

For many people, marriage is the most central, defining relationship in their lives. Whom we marry and how we nurture that relationship can affect the course of our lives immensely. And marriage is hard. Even when it's good, stable, and rewarding for both partners, marriage requires work, sacrifice, compromise, and attentiveness. We should keep this in mind to make sure we do not grow complacent in our own relationships and also because it points to the fact that there are valid reasons why many marriages don't make it. And those who suffer through a divorce should not be judged but rather lifted up because they've been through so much already. Too many people who go through a divorce feel lonely, judged, and isolated, which makes their experience even worse.

There are solid, dependable foundations upon which healthy relationships and marriages must be based: honesty, trust, selflessness, sacrifice, compromise, patience, and forgiveness. Falling in love is easy; staying in love takes work. It should also be fun, meaningful, energizing, and comforting; but like most things that can give us so much, that doesn't mean work isn't part of the equation.

It is not surprising that as our culture has become more self-centered, more and more relationships seem to struggle. But we can resist this by remembering what relationships need and how important they are for us. Building all our meaningful relationships, and especially marriage, on the right foundations will help ensure their stability and longevity for the future. Being self-critical and checking that these foundations are in place and well-maintained is essential because the quality of our lives is always directly tied to the quality of our relationships. The happiest and most fulfilled people in life have figured this out and live it out every day.

CHAPTER 17

Faith

Many misunderstandings persist in our culture around what it means to live a life of faith. This question lies at the heart of theology, a field that will never be exhausted. Having faith in God does not mean that everything in life will work out just the way we plan or that we will be spared hardship and pain, tragedy and suffering. It does not mean that there is a master puppeteer in the sky, orchestrating our every move. We do have free will, and bad things do happen to us all. Pain and suffering are realities for every person. So, given all of this, what is faith, and what does it mean to be a person of faith? Why does it matter whether or not we live in faith?

The writer of the Epistle to the Hebrews gives this definition: "Faith is the assurance of things hoped for, the conviction of things not seen" (Hebrews 11:1). According to these words, faith and hope are intertwined, two sides of the same coin, perhaps inseparable. In a similar vein, Augustine is to have said, "Faith is to believe what you do not see; the reward of this faith is to see what you believe." Another example is said to be from Thomas Aquinas who wrote, "To one who has faith, no explanation is necessary; to one without faith, no explanation is possible." So faith can change how we see things, what makes intuitive sense for us. And Charles Spurgeon preached that "faith obliterates time, annihilates distance, and brings future things at once into its possession."[1] Faith can change the meaning of history, of far-off events and ideas, as well as the future.

The truth is, there is no singular, definitive understanding of faith. These thinkers all draw on the same traditions and are worshipping the same God, and so there is considerable overlap and agreement, but they also have their own distinctive ideas and points of emphasis. Part of faith, too, is having confidence that people across the world and throughout history can contemplate this one God, read the same Bible, and come away from both with different ideas and understandings that are still part of the same tradition, the same faith.

Most generally, I'd say that faith is a way of being, a way of living, a way of approaching the future. It involves being always open to the Spirit. Faith is what gives us courage in the face of fear and hope in the face of disappointment. Faith is trusting that life will go on and can change dramatically, even after bad things happen. Faith means learning to not be trapped or owned by things that have happened in the past. The past should not and does not define us. Guilt and shame can be overcome, no matter how insurmountable they may seem.

Faith is learning to see the world through a new and different lens. It's not an escape from reality but a refusal to accept that what we see with unaided eyes is all there is, for there is always more to this world. There is more than we can see and more than we can know. There are secrets of how and why in the world that only God seems to have the key to. But faith also means we can be sure that our actions do, in fact, matter. Faith means believing

What the World Needs Now

that we can leave the world better than we found it and that God wants us to do this.

Faith involves not getting bogged down by the trivial things in life, the things that really don't matter in the big picture. Living in faith means moving beyond a world of superficiality, materialism, resentment, and control. It means looking for the deeper meaning that is all around us, in the world and in our relationships; it means embracing the grand mystery of creation and the joy of everyday existence.

Living in faith means reminding ourselves that we are all on a journey and we simply don't know or control the future. Our faith gives us hope in this future—hope that things will be better, that God's designs for the world may more fully come into being, that we may grow to be more fulfilled and Spirit-filled people, and that we may help others do the same. And as we step into this future, we are called to live out the kind of character that our faith entails, practicing humility, gratitude, love, and presence every step of the way.

CHAPTER 18

Connection

Social isolation, loneliness, anxiety, and depression are growing challenges in the twenty-first century. The internet and now social media were born into a culture in which traditional forms of community were breaking down due to a variety of factors. In the book *Lost Connections: Uncovering the Real Causes of Depression—and the Unexpected Solutions*, journalist Johann Hari makes the case that the rising rates of anxiety and depression in our culture may not simply be tied to chemical imbalances in the brain. He does not completely dismiss that possibility, but he argues that there are multiple factors that have contributed to this rise, all related to communal fragmentation.

In writing the book, Hari talked to multiple psychologists around the world who have done extensive research on the subjects of anxiety, depression, and social connection, including neuroscience researcher John Cacioppo. Hari writes, "Cacioppo told me the evidence is clear: social media can't compensate us psychologically for what we have lost—social life. More than that—our obsessive use of social media is an attempt to fill a hole, a great hallowing, that took place before anyone had a smartphone."[1]

Clearly, big tech companies found a way to tap into this void and have made billions of dollars in the process. Folks like Steve Jobs and Mark Zuckerberg realized that this is both a spiritual

What the World Needs Now

crisis and a relationship crisis. But are we any better off now that we have all of these gadgets and social media platforms? I would argue that the situation is even worse because screen time is not a real substitute for the authentic community that was previously found in churches, civic clubs, PTAs, and twelve-step groups. Hari also points out that as our society has become less communal and more fragmented, our culture has become more materialistic. Why? It's the way we compete with one another and send messages about our own status and importance to others. Rather than connect with one another, we find ourselves wanting to one-up one another.

Hari consulted American psychologist Tim Kassar, who says, "All of us have certain innate needs—to feel connected, to feel valued, to feel secure, to feel we make a difference in the world, to have autonomy, to feel we are good at something."[2] These needs and desires are universal ones that we all share. But our culture has somehow managed to convince us that we will meet these basic human needs through money and material goods. What we now see is a materialistic society full of lonely people who still long for human connection. We try to accumulate stuff to impress other people only to find out that we still don't (and never will) have enough stuff. Authentic connection must always be based on who we are and not on what we have. Values and relationships will always be more important than money and things. Too many people get this entirely backward.

A number of years ago, I got a phone call on a Sunday afternoon. It was from a wealthy businessman in my church.

Connection

That morning, I had referred to the epidemic of loneliness in our culture and how many people have plenty to live with but are looking for something to live for. This person was basically calling to tell me he was lonely. He had achieved incredible wealth and success. He had traveled the world. He had bought and sold many companies. He had homes all over the country. But he honestly did not know if his family loved him for who he was or for the lifestyle he had provided for them. What a difficult place to be!

This kind of cautionary tale highlights the vital importance of seeking connection and developing relationships, especially with those you are closest to. Too many people realize too late that there is no substitute for these relationships; they have to be protected and nurtured above all else in life. Money and success only matter if you get to enjoy it with the people whom you love and care about. If you sacrifice your family and friendships along the way, it's simply not worth it.

CHAPTER 19

Gratitude

We must learn to acknowledge the fundamental difference between envy and gratitude, coveting and contentment. We live in a culture with an economic system that, to some degree, fuels itself on coveting and wanting what others already have. We are told over and over again by marketers and advertisers that we deserve things that are bigger, better, and nicer than what we already have. We are told that we would be so much happier if we just went out and bought whatever it is they are promoting because we deserve it. We are told that the American dream is predicated on the idea of having a better life than the previous generation. We don't just want to give our kids what we had—we want to give them something better. All of this makes gratitude and contentment very challenging today.

Making things worse, through social media, most people constantly run a well-monitored highlight reel of their life. And then we wonder why we are never satisfied and why we remain restless and discontented. A study done at Harvard University over a seventy-five-year period tracked 268 male students who graduated from Harvard College between the years 1938 and 1940, men who have now mostly passed away, in order to find out what makes for a happy and meaningful life over the long haul.[1] What they discovered is that love is what matters most; connection to other people and forming friendships and good relationships makes for a meaningful and well-lived life. The research further found that money and power, although important in achieving business success, do not necessarily equate to more happiness unless they are accompanied by the other things that bring us love, connection, and joy.

Duke theologians Stanley Hauerwas and Will Willimon once said, "Our problem as humans is not that we are full of desire, aflame with unfulfillment. Our problem is that we long for that which is unfulfilling. We attempt to be content with that which can never satisfy.... What we want is power and status. Alas, we find that no matter what we have acquired, there is always someone we envy."[2] We all have a God-sized hole in our heart, and we throw everything under the sun at it—sex, money, power, status, alcohol, drugs, you name it. Nothing can fill it once and for all. Only a deep spirituality and connection with God can take away the restlessness.

We should heed the words of the apostle Paul and focus on the good things of life. "Whatever is true, whatever is honorable, whatever is just, whatever is pure, whatever is pleasing, whatever is commendable, if there is any excellence and if there is anything worthy of praise, think about these things" (Philippians 4:8). There is too much negativity and not enough gratitude in our culture and our common character. Paul continues, "I have learned to be content with whatever I have. I know what it is to have little, and I know what it is to have plenty" (Philippians 4:11-12). Genuine gratitude for what we already have can help eliminate fear and anxiety, envy and jealousy and lead us to a life of contentment. We should be grateful for our families and our

What the World Needs Now

health. We should be grateful for our jobs and our friends. We should be grateful for our homes and food to eat. We should be grateful for the gift of each new day because we simply do not know how long our lives will last. Living with gratitude is a conscious choice that we make every single day. Rather than focusing on what is missing, we should focus on our blessings and do everything we can to not take them for granted.

Our family made a trip last year to Guatemala, where our church has a strong ministry presence. We have sponsored hundreds of children and built over eighty homes there in recent years. What amazes me every time I visit is how much joy the people have. They are living in poverty, with very few material possessions, yet they are happy and grateful. I compare that to those of us here in the United States who have many blessings but take them for granted and find reasons to complain and desire still more. Gratitude is a choice, a worldview, and a way of approaching life. Sometimes, it takes seeing the lives of people in radically different circumstances from your own to fully understand the life-changing power of gratitude.

CHAPTER 20
Civility

Before his death in the fall of 2020, Rabbi Jonathan Sacks expressed his deep concern about the death of civility in Western culture. Not only has this become an enormous problem in the secular realm of political dialogue and the public square but it is also a significant concern among believers of the same faith tradition. "Civility is more than good manners," he writes. "It is a recognition that violent speech leads to violent deeds; that listening respectfully to your opponent is a necessary part of the politics of a free society; and that liberal democracy, predicated as it is on the dignity of diversity, must keep the peace between contending groups by honoring us all equally, in both our diversity and our commonalities."[1]

Sacks was purposively specific about the fundamental reasons why civility has declined so rapidly. First, we have seen a deepening sense of individualism that has grown in Western culture ever since the 1960s. While there are positive aspects of this development, it has also meant that we have moved further and further away from the civic mindset of the Greatest Generation, who invested heavily in social capital in the wake of World War II. Second, the internet has become a major cultural force, which has permanently altered the way that we acquire information. We are living in an age of information overload, and much of what we are exposed to is inaccurate or not grounded in fact. Third, and perhaps most significantly, we are experiencing the decivilizing impact of social media, often described as the disinhibition effect that arises when communication is anonymous, asynchronous, depersonalized, and remote. People will type and post things they would never say face-to-face to another person. According to Sacks, this amounts to a "cacophony of noise in place of true communication." The more outrageous the comment, the more views and "likes" it might get, or at least the more attention it might receive. Fourth, we are experiencing a significant divide in our culture between the "somewheres" and the "anywheres." This is the growing gap between the haves and have-nots, coastal elites and small towners, those who benefit from the new economy and those who get left behind and deeply resent it. This divide is real and creates serious resentment.[2]

All of these factors have contributed to the decline of civility in our contemporary culture. It seems like one of the great challenges for people of all faith traditions is to try to lead us out of the wilderness and back to a place where we respect one another's humanity and differences. Sadly, however, Christians often exhibit the same division, hostility, and disunity as the rest of the culture—a far cry from Christ's final prayer in Gethsemane that "they may all be one . . . so that the world may believe" (John 17:21). This presents us with one of the great challenges of our day. Will people of faith rise to meet it? But how can we even begin to address these issues?

Sacks offers three "principles of civility" that he believes would go a long way in making this problem better. First, for there to be justice, all sides must be heard. Our legal system should always seek to honor this. Second, truth on earth cannot aspire to be truth as it is in heaven. All truth on earth represents but one perspective, and there are multiple perspectives; everybody's life, experience, and worldview are different. Third, the alternative to argument is violence, which is why argument and conversation must never cease. We have all seen what happens when it does.

When civility dissipates, a new world of problems arises. New divisions can appear. People who agree on the fundamentals can get lost on the details they dispute. Compromise and collaboration become increasingly difficult. The goal of returning to civility is not to change somebody else's mind but to build healthier relationships, foster community, learn from one another, and have meaningful dialogue.

CHAPTER 21

Leadership

Leadership is not for the faint of heart. It takes passion, conviction, nerve, a thick skin, and resilience. F. Washington Jarvis says, "Leaders are caught in a catch-22. If a leader is strong, undeterred by projection, blame, and calumny, he is then labeled as arrogant, authoritarian, dictatorial. If he sets aside his initiatives, goes with the way the wind is blowing, if he backs down at all, he or she is immediately labeled as 'weak' and 'a waffler.'"[1] Leadership is always challenging, and many people are not up for the challenge.

Throughout my life, I have learned a great deal about leadership simply by watching other leaders. People like John C. Maxwell, Andy Stanley, Rick Warren, and others have shaped my personal understanding of leadership. Not all leadership styles are the same because not all leaders are the same. Jesus was one of the greatest leaders to ever live because of his willingness to serve and put others first. He demonstrated that spiritual leadership always involves service and self-sacrifice.

There are many in our culture who want to be leaders but aren't willing to pay the price. They don't know what it entails. Many want the recognition and prestige without the responsibility, the glory without the hard work. But leadership is not an end unto itself; it takes courage, always involves opening

Leadership

oneself up to criticism, and is often costly. One of the best books I have read on leadership is Edwin Friedman's *Failure of Nerve*, which shows how leaders fail when they lose heart and give in to anxiety.[2] Anxiety is a constant threat that all effective leaders must learn how to navigate. We live in a particularly anxious culture, so leaders need to be attuned to what is and is not worth worrying about.

Further, anybody who wants to lead must pay attention to their spiritual tank. If the tank is empty or close to it, leadership will be very difficult if not impossible. Far too many people are trying to lead on empty. That simply does not work; it leads to burnout, rash decisions, and a lack of keen insight. Self-care matters tremendously if leaders are to remain healthy and effective.

While there are a number of different leadership styles that can work in different situations, and good leaders can display a range of personality types, there is a set of characteristics that most of them will possess. Effective spiritual leaders should have these six core traits:

1. *Character*. It's who you are that matters. Character is formed over time, and the foundation is laid early in life. We all fall short at times, but character is built up through the trials and tribulations of life. Patterns of behavior matter.
2. *Courage*. Nobody can lead anything without having the courage to do so. Why? Leaders are

criticized all the time. Courage combined with resilience will make all the difference.

3. *A positive attitude.* Nobody wants to follow a cynic who is always negative and pessimistic. True leaders always inspire hope and focus on the good.

4. *Teachability.* Life is a classroom, and we must never stop learning and growing. Once you stop learning, you can no longer lead. This involves being able to listen empathetically to the concerns of others.

5. *Ability to form relationships.* Effective leaders surround themselves with other leaders and form relationships with those they lead. Trust is built in the process as the currency of relationships. This is true in the church, business, education, politics, and any other field. The heathiest spiritual leaders form and maintain strong relationships.

6. *Humility.* Leaders must work to overcome pride and maintain a deep sense of humility. Being wrong and apologizing are always signs of strength. Leaders should be willing to give their team credit for success and accomplishments.

Although it has never been easy, leadership is especially taxing and difficult in today's culture. So it is all the more important to emphasize that leaders are called to cultivate strong inner character and integrity. This takes time, so leaders will need

Leadership

to have the endurance required to learn hard lessons over time. They must find courage in the face of overwhelming challenges and threats. They need to find ways to remain hopeful with a positive attitude when others become negative and cynical. And they must never stop learning and cultivating a genuine humility along the way. Leaders must never stop learning and working to cultivate these traits.

CHAPTER 22

Money

Legend has it that in 1923, a meeting of America's most powerful men took place at the Edgewater Beach Hotel in Chicago. Collectively, these tycoons controlled more wealth than there was in the United States Treasury, and for years newspapers and magazines had been printing their success stories and urging the youth of the nation to follow their examples. This is what had happened to seven of the men:

- The president of the largest independent steel company, Charles Schwab, lived on borrowed money the last five years of his life and died broke.
- The country's greatest wheat speculator, Arthur Cutten, died abroad insolvent.
- The president of the New York Stock Exchange, Richard Whitney, served a term in Sing Sing prison.
- A member of the president's cabinet, Albert Fall, was pardoned from prison so he could die at home.
- The "Wall Street Bear," Jesse Livermore, committed suicide.
- The president of the Bank of International Settlements, Leon Fraser, committed suicide.
- The head of the world's greatest monopoly, Ivar Kreuger, committed suicide.[1]

Money

All of these men had learned how to make money and be successful, but not one of them had learned how to live. Here's the truth: Jesus is concerned with motive, values, and the quality of our relationships to ourselves and others. That is what matters for a happy life, not how much money or power you have.

Friedrich Nietzsche lived during the second half of the nineteenth century and was known as a pessimistic nihilist who was hostile to Christianity and conventional morality. However, he was also very intelligent and once made a prediction that should haunt all people of faith. Nietzsche famously said that one day, money will replace God in Western culture.[2] If we take a look around, for many people today, Nietzsche's prediction seems to already be proven true. Money is perhaps the number one object of idolatry in the world. In truth, some people are much more concerned about net worth than self-worth.

For many, life seems like one big competition to see who can acquire the biggest, shiniest, most expensive new toys. Those who have money and means are often admired and respected. Those who don't have money are looked down upon. But there is a shallowness to it all that any honest person can see.

Jesus was aware of the dangers of a materialistic mindset, so he addressed it often throughout his ministry. He said, "You cannot serve God and wealth" (Matthew 6:24). One or the other always wins out. He also raises a profound question that every generation should ask: "What will it profit them if they gain the whole world but forfeit their life?" (Matthew 16:26). We can reframe this question in more modern, practical terms: What does it profit you to build a huge company if you

What the World Needs Now

lose your marriage in the process? What does it profit you to be a workaholic if you miss all your children's games and plays? What does it profit you to become a multimillionaire if you have no true friends left in your life, only the hangers-on?

To be clear, there is nothing wrong with being successful and making money. We all must do it to survive. And there is nothing wrong with being wealthy as long as your values are strong and clear. But how can we prevent our culture from becoming one in which money matters more than character? Many people seem to get a character pass simply because they are rich. Jesus warned against this (Matthew 16:26).

So how should we live today? What aspects of our character can help us be effective stewards of our money, put it to good use, and allow it to have a positive effect on our relationships? Here are three suggestions:

1. *Be grateful.* Be grateful for what we have, grateful for our many blessings, grateful for the people in our lives. If we spend our entire lives always wanting more, we will never be satisfied and we will never enjoy what we have. A lack of gratitude leads to constant restlessness and the insatiable desire for more and more. And if we're not grateful for what we have right now, what makes us believe we will be grateful once we get the things we want?

2. *Be generous.* Be generous with our time, generous with our talent, generous with our money. We all have the ability to make a difference in this world but only if we make the investment. There is a

lot of need, there are a lot of hopeless situations, and we all have the ability to give back and be generous. And true generosity does not result in loss or regret; on the contrary, it can be extremely liberating and fulfilling. Holding on tightly to everything you have only smothers your spirit.

3. *Be fearless.* So many people hoard their money and their possessions out of fear—fear that they won't have enough, fear that it will run out, fear that others will have more, fear that they'll feel inadequate. But fearful is no way to live. It takes the joy out of life and keeps a person focused on themself.

CHAPTER 23

Wisdom

One Monday afternoon a few years ago, I sat around the boardroom table at our church with about twenty older, wiser, and largely retired men from our church, most of them in their seventies or eighties. I was interested in picking their brains about life and what they have learned throughout the years. I am convinced that many in the younger generations do not take the time to soak up wisdom from those who now have the advantage of reflecting upon their lives. They have fought the battles and learned the lessons, and they have the scars and character to prove it. My two questions to them were simple and straightforward: What is your best life advice for the next generation? Do you have any regrets? Here are some of wise pieces of advice that were shared that day.

Seek God first and develop a spiritual life at a young age. Don't work too hard at the expense of your family. Find the sacred balance between work and family. Enjoy every stage of life as it comes because it goes by all too quickly and you can't turn back the clock.

Be kind to everyone because kindness is a form of love. Treat others the way you want to be treated. Make faith a priority in your marriage and family life. Be proud but not prideful, confident but not arrogant. Maturity comes with years.

Wisdom

Disappointment is inevitable. Be gentle and compassionate. Try to become somebody that you will admire.

Be optimistic and positive. Don't dwell too much on the past, which you cannot change. Learn to enjoy what you're doing so you never have to work a day in your life. Guard your reputation and don't compromise your character. Stay focused on meaningful objectives and live with the end in mind.

Beware of seeking instant gratification. Many of the things worth doing take a long and sustained effort. Lead by example. Don't ask others to do things you wouldn't do. Be humble and keep your ego in check. Learn to live within your means. Money is not the answer to everything.

Remember that relationships matter most so learn to nurture them and invest in them. Take nothing for granted and beware of developing an entitlement mindset. Spend quality time with your children because they will grow up fast. Carve out regular time to nurture the soul. Travel with your family whenever possible to make memories that will last forever. Give it your all, whether at work or at home. Follow the example set by Christ.

Take care of your health at a young age because it only gets more challenging. Marry somebody who can put you in your place whenever necessary. Cultivate friendships that will last a lifetime.

Tell the truth, even when it's hard and inconvenient. Be true to yourself and be the same person no matter who you might be around. Love others even when they've hurt you, and

What the World Needs Now

don't forget the importance of forgiveness and letting things go. Approach every day as a gift because we never know about tomorrow. Don't worry constantly and needlessly. Trust that things will turn out okay, even if it's not what you had planned.

I'm deeply grateful to these men for their wisdom and insight. My hope and prayer is that younger generations will continue to learn and gain wisdom from those who have gone before us.

CHAPTER 24

Priorities

Scottie Scheffler is one of the top golfers in the world. In the spring of 2024, he and his wife, Meredith, were expecting their first child. He made the headlines at the Masters when he announced that should his wife go into labor while he was playing in the tournament, he would withdraw from the tournament, even if he was in the lead, to go and be present when the baby was born. Fortunately, Meredith didn't go into labor. And Scheffler won the Masters Tournament as well as the next PGA Tour event, held the following weekend. He is one of the best in the world, but his priorities and values are clearly in line.

Life is a constant series of decisions about what is most important and what is not as significant. Sometimes we get it right, sometimes we don't. Many people say that they have certain values and priorities, but many of the decisions that they make do not align with those values. You may have observed or experienced some of these situations in your own life:

- Some say that their marriage is important, but they don't intentionally carve out time to be just with their spouse.
- Some say their children are important, but they often work late and miss many of the games and plays and then wonder how they grew up so fast.

What the World Needs Now

- Some say that their physical health is important, but they don't eat well, get enough sleep, or exercise.
- Some say that their friendships are important, but they rarely reach out to check in and see how their friends are doing.
- Some say that their mental and emotional health are important, but they don't go to counseling, seek out a spiritual director, or take time to renew, rest, and refresh.
- Some say their faith is important, but they don't pray, read Scripture, serve others, join a small group, or come to a church and support it.

Now, of course, none of these things is easy or without compromise. Being present for children when you have work, friends, and other priorities always involves trade-offs. Just finding time for exercise can be daunting, let alone doing it. And God is patient, ever-present, and merciful, so maybe deepening our faith can wait. Right?

I once attended a course that was called "Managing Yourself and Leading Others." What became clear in our class discussion is that leadership always begins with self. Some people want to be in charge of others, but they have a difficult time controlling themselves. This is why self-reflection and inner work are always necessary.

In leading a large church, I have found that every day brings new obstacles and challenges—staff conflicts, church politics, disagreements, you name it—that have the potential to take me to a nonspiritual place. I simply cannot let that happen.

I must set boundaries and protect my time to read, write, pray, and build relationships with my leaders so that I can do the main part of my job well.

Every day, our decisions should be made based on our well-considered and thought-out priorities. We need to know what matters most and what deserves our greatest attention. Priorities can certainly change over time, but we must always be aware of what we should focus on first, perhaps what is most pressing or enables us to tackle everything else in the most effective way. When we don't know our priorities, we get pulled in a thousand different directions and end up not doing anything particularly well. We become a mile wide and an inch deep. We become distracted and we start to major in the minors.

Many in our culture will say they want to grow spiritually, emotionally, and in their faith, but if their weekly or daily schedule is looked at even briefly, it's clear that no time is set aside for this to happen. And it does need time and intentional effort. But so often, one activity leads to another and then to another. Busyness and overcommitment have become a badge of honor. Americans are indeed busy, but what are we busy doing? God is indeed patient and forgiving, as we should be with both others and ourselves. But we also need to carve out time to work on our relationship with God. Making God a priority helps us center ourselves, which clears up the clutter in our lives and allows what is truly most important to rise to the top of our lists.

CHAPTER 25
Diversity

So far, the twenty-first century has been marked by growing polarization and hostility in the United States and specifically within American Christianity. Christians have proven time and time again that we are very good at fighting with one another. Denominations continue to divide over the same issues. This causes many to leave the church and give up on organized religion entirely. At what point will the church and our society understand the need for civility and faithful disagreement over controversial issues? Many will say that the church has ignored its real mission in order to battle over the culture wars. There is probably some truth to that. Social issues seem to come to the forefront and overshadow many other equally or more important matters. And the way we talk about these issues becomes so clouded by argument, accusation, and exaggeration that we hardly know what is actually important anymore.

Diversity, for example, is hotly debated in this day and age. What do we mean by the term *diversity*? There are so many different types of diversity: racial, socioeconomic, theological, generational, political. All of these areas are relevant to the discussion. But I find it interesting that for many, racial diversity is the only one that seems to matter. Wokeness, in one form or another, has risen and fallen in our institutions and news headlines. DEI offices have been opened and then shut down.

Diversity

The Supreme Court ruled against affirmative action by saying that the answer to decades of systemic racism is not more systemic racism.

Political polarization is also very real and has shifted the character of many institutions. Many churches are now divided along partisan lines. Mike Slaughter, Charles Gutenson, and Robert Jones published a fascinating book in 2012 titled *Hijacked: Responding to the Partisan Church Divide*. They write, "Why is it, then, that we have allowed political partisanship to enter so deeply into our churches? And, perhaps more importantly, how is it that we have allowed those differences to divide us, to create obstacles among us, and to have created an environment in which one or the other can be somehow considered less a 'follower of Jesus' simply on the basis of one being the supporter of a particular party or ideology."[1]

It should be abundantly clear by now that discipleship, partisanship, and social positions do not line up neatly. According to Slaughter, Gutenson, and Jones, "One can be theologically conservative and politically conservative; one can be theologically liberal and politically conservative; one can be theologically conservative and politically liberal; and one can be theologically liberal and politically liberal."[2] Therefore, simply throwing around the terms "liberal" and "conservative" is often not very helpful. It can actually be part of the problem. Yet these words are deeply imbedded into our American vocabulary and way of thinking. We all want to size one another up, and these categories offer a powerful but sometimes deceptive shortcut.

What the World Needs Now

In *The Happiness Hypothesis*, social psychologist Jonathan Haidt shows that both liberals and conservatives make valuable contributions to society based on their different interests and passions. As Haidt says, "Liberals are experts in thinking about issues of victimization, equality, autonomy, and the rights of individuals, particularly those of minorities and nonconformists. Conservatives, on the other hand, are experts in thinking about loyalty to the group, respect for authority and tradition, and sacredness. When one side overwhelms the other, the results are likely to be ugly. A society without liberals would be harsh and oppressive to many individuals. A society without conservatives would lose many of the social structures and constraints that Durkheim showed are so valuable."[3] This is also the case in the church, which demonstrates the ongoing need for mutual respect and healthy dialogue among all groups. We can and should learn from one another. We need one another to be a stronger and more complete church, with a range of talents, abilities, and strengths.

Christians are perhaps as unsuccessful as any at being able to disagree passionately while still maintaining fellowship with those with whom we disagree. Many ministers desperately long to see this happen more often in the church. I have had people leave our church because they thought we were too conservative. I have had people leave our church because they thought we were too liberal. We need to look for unity in the things essential to the faith. We need to allow diversity of opinion on things that are not essential and not be threatened by disagreement.

Diversity

But regardless of whether we agree or disagree on any given topic, Christ calls us to model love, civility, and decency for one another. We are called to see beyond political labels, race, and class, looking through the eyes of the heart. Living with balance, holding the tension, and having the dialogue will always be important for the church and, really, for any institution.

And we must also remember that Christian leadership involves service as a key component. That is the way that Christ led, serving others. We cannot ask others to do something that we are not willing to do. Christ's call in our lives is to be selfless in a culture that is often selfish and self-centered. Disparate groups and voices should seek to collaborate and work together. This involves dialogue, listening, and compromise. Compromise is called for in any diverse culture. And for us, it seems necessary, as Christ calls us to lead and make decisions that are in the best interest of all and not just a few.

CHAPTER 26

Habits

In 1989, Stephen R. Covey published *The Seven Habits of Highly Effective People*. It has become a classic in the business and leadership community, challenging and influencing millions of people across the globe to adopt these vital strategies:

- *Be proactive.* Take initiative and don't live life in a reactive mode.
- *Begin with the end in mind.* Know where you want to be in the future and then move toward it. Make decisions that move you toward your goal.
- *Put first things first.* Know what your priorities are as well as what is urgent and what is not.
- *Think win-win.* Seek solutions in life where both parties win and the results are mutually beneficial.
- *Seek first to understand, then to be understood.* Empathy, listening, and understanding go a long way in relationships. Loneliness abounds and many want to know if you care or not.
- *Synergize!* Use teamwork and complementary skills to get the job done.
- *Sharpen the saw.* Never stop learning, growing, developing, and searching.[1]

These are certainly valuable pieces of advice in almost any context. There's a reason why Covey's book has sold tens of millions of copies.

But what if we wanted to come up with a list of the seven habits of highly *spiritual* people? I have some ideas.

- *Be disciplined*. Carve out time every day for prayer, meditation, reading, and stillness. Disconnect from the ongoing noise and disruptions of the world. This should also include disconnecting from technology.
- *Keep the big picture in mind*. Human beings can get very worked up over things that really don't matter in the big picture.
- *Live your priorities*. Good is the enemy of great. Don't let the small and petty stuff rule the day. Know what matters most and choose to focus on those things first. If you don't get to other things that are less important, so be it.
- *Treat others the way you want to be treated*. Always imagine what it would be like to be on the receiving end of your words and actions. Jesus taught this. Some people would be shocked to learn how they treat and speak to others.
- *Show kindness, empathy, and compassion*. Everybody is fighting some type of battle in life. We usually do not know what it is. Life is difficult, challenging, and stressful.
- *Form meaningful relationships with people who make you better*. The company you keep will pull you up or down. Be around people who influence you for the better. Surround yourself with people who will give you support and honest feedback.

What the World Needs Now

- *Avoid getting angry whenever possible or deal with anger in healthy ways.* Anger, resentment, and bitterness take us away from our spiritual center. These things also heavily affect our physical, mental, and emotional health. Anger makes us say and do things that we regret.

Instilling these habits can have many wide-ranging effects when they are practiced and cultivated over time. This is how highly spiritual people find a way to remain cool, calm, and collected in the face of stress and difficulty. The truth is, however, we live in a world where most people believe that the spiritual life is important but very few are serious about intentionally doing what it takes to grow spiritually. In his recent book *Practicing the Way*, John Mark Comer asks, "Would the people who know you best say you are becoming more loving, joyful, and at peace? More patient and less frustrated? Kinder, gentler, softening with time and pervaded by goodness? Faithful, especially in hard times, and self-controlled?"[2] These are important questions for us to ask if we want to take our spiritual life seriously. The world is busy, loud, chaotic, and nonstop. It can be stressful and more often provokes anxiety than the peace we seek. But Jesus reminds us where to look: "Peace I leave with you; my peace I give to you. I do not give to you as the world gives" (John 14:27). To make time for God, find this peace, and allow it to infuse all our thoughts and actions, we must be intentional in our habits, our focus, our choices, and in how we structure our time each day.

CHAPTER 27

Purpose

For many years now, we have been experiencing a tragic crisis of opioid addiction in our nation that has claimed many lives. The bottom line is there are many in our culture who lack a sense of meaning and purpose, and they are doing whatever it takes to make the pain of this lack go away. The statistics are simply staggering, and the death toll keeps rising. So what does it mean to live life and cultivate a sense of purpose?

I was once at a leadership conference where I heard John C. Maxwell present a threefold definition of success: First, know your purpose. Second, grow to your maximum potential. Third, sow seeds that benefit others.[1] If we stick with the first part of this definition, we cannot help acknowledging that many people do not know their purpose or live their lives with a sense of purpose. And when you have no clear sense of purpose, meaninglessness and emptiness worm their way in. Addiction can easily fill the void as well. I try to always keep some big, important questions at the forefront of my mind: What motivates people? What gives people drive? What gives us purpose? Because until we can answer these questions for ourselves, we are simply going through the motions, staying busy, and life has little meaning.

People have different ideas about what the purpose of life is or should be. Some think it is to make as much money as you can or as many connections as you can. Some say the purpose of

What the World Needs Now

life is to give your children things you didn't have. Others think it is simply to keep your head above water and survive.

I think the meaning and purpose of life is much deeper and much more profound than any of these things: We are here to love and to be loved. We are here to worship God and not false idols. We are here to put others before ourselves. We are here to build healthy relationships based on authenticity and trust. We are here to lift one another up when life beats us down and to look out for those who have little or nothing. We are here to show mercy and compassion and practice forgiveness and grace. We are here to serve and to leave the world better than we found it.

Rick Warren begins his famous book *The Purpose Driven Life* with a profound statement that points at a common thread among all the things I just listed: "It's not about you!"[2] So in a world that has become increasingly selfish, narcissistic, materialistic, and often shallow, should it be a surprise that opioid addiction is now out of control? We discover our meaning and purpose when we move beyond ourselves, when we look to the world to see how our passion and skill can address needs of others. Discovering our purpose in life can be one of the most liberating things to ever happen. Until we learn how to do this, meaninglessness, restlessness, and emptiness will remain very real threats in our lives.

CHAPTER 28

Hope

On the Friday of Labor Day weekend, September 2, 2005, my mother took her own life. I unwillingly joined a club I never wanted to be in—suicide survivors. I was numb for a long time. What else could we have done? How did this happen? She was the proverbial life of the party until her depression took over. I think about all the life she missed out on—weddings, grandchildren, birthdays, graduations, friendships. She had a long battle with severe depression that led to a state of utter hopelessness. I certainly wish her life had played out differently. Today, some twenty years on, I still miss her and think about her often.

Many people who make the decision to take their own lives are in a very dark place. Many are ill, suffering from a mental condition that renders them incapable of enjoying life the way others do. They simply want the pain to stop and to go away. Many feel like they won't be missed and the world would be just fine without them. Thankfully, these illnesses are becoming less stigmatized in our culture, which enables people to more easily and readily seek the help they need through counseling, medication, and a variety of other means. More often than not, people can receive help that genuinely improves their lives, sometimes dramatically.

Young people, in particular, need to know that they are loved, supported, and treasured. They don't have to handle all the challenges of life alone. Parents should communicate with them

What the World Needs Now

openly and often. Counselors will tell you that anxiety is now at an all-time high, leading many to feel completely overwhelmed and discouraged. And at the same time, loneliness has become an epidemic. Social psychologist Jonathan Haidt says that real happiness does not come from getting or achieving, it does not come from within, but it comes from meaningful connections with others because we are social creatures. So those who work toward developing meaningful relationships in life seem to be more satisfied and fulfilled. We were just not designed to live in isolation. Hope is found in community, which enables us to recognize that others do care and are there in our time of need.

What keeps people like my mother from finding hope? Mental illness is surely one answer to that question. But there are others as well. We lose hope when we retreat and lose our connection with others. We lose hope when we forget that life is a team sport that we have to do together. We all wrestle with the same challenges, the same stresses, the same fears, so we must learn to share them with one another and draw support from one another. Otherwise, feelings of isolation and helplessness lead to despair and emptiness. If this goes far enough, there may be no escape.

There is no need to judge those who have taken their own lives. But we should all work to prevent others from doing the same thing by helping create a world where people no longer feel isolated and helpless, shouldering life's burdens by themselves. Reach out to those who are hurting. Let them know they are not alone. Pay close attention to those around you because somebody you love dearly may be struggling in ways you might never imagine.

CHAPTER 29

Simplicity

I have had the opportunity to minister to and become close friends with several businessmen who have served as CEOs of very large companies. They are smart, motivated, highly successful, and have accomplished a lot in their various fields. However, I have always been impressed by the ones who are able to walk away from their careers sooner rather than later. Why? Because they realize that there is more to life than grinding it out, making money, and achieving success. They want to give back and lead in other areas. They want to travel. They want to spend more time with their spouses, children, and grandchildren. They want to slow down, be less stressed, take care of their health, and enjoy whatever years they have left. Some put all that off until it is too late.

In America, we often believe the myth that you are what you do. When we meet new people, we often ask, "What do you do?" But what somebody does only tells us part of their story, sometimes a very small part. It really doesn't tell us who they are or what matters most to them. I have known many men (and some women) who try to retire only to find that they are completely lost without their career. They let their career define them. That's not a healthy way to live. Life is about much more than work, as important as work might be.

What the World Needs Now

Sometimes busyness does not equal success, and more is not always better. Sometimes we have to slow down and see the bigger picture in life so our priorities remain rightly ordered.

What are the things that matter most in your life? Where do you spend the majority of your time, your energy, and your money? What are you most passionate about? What motivates you? What do you consider to be the foundation of your life?

We all have to decide for ourselves what our priorities are going to be, and then we have to make sure that the majority of our time and energy is devoted to things that we say are most important. Knowing what our priorities should be is one thing, but it's another to actually live out those priorities from day to day.

We all have to make these decisions for ourselves, to decide what is most important and most deserving of our time and energy. But I have some pretty clear ideas about my own priorities. Thinking about how best to incorporate these into my daily life and work has been the best way for me to live a life of peace and simplicity.

FAITH

In a quotation often attributed to Jimmy Carter, he says "I have one life and one chance to make it count for something. I'm free to choose what that something is, and the something I've chosen is my faith. Now, my faith goes beyond theology and religion and requires considerable work and effort. My faith demands—this is not optional—that I do whatever I can, wherever I am, whenever I can, for as long as I can with all that I have…to try to make a difference."

In order to make faith a priority in our lives, we have to be committed and disciplined. And, of course, we have to become active believers. Faith is not just something that we possess; it's something that we do. God calls us to live out our faith each and every day. One of the best ways that we can do that is by being around other Christians because faith is "much better caught than it is taught." We must take the time every week to read our Bible because God speaks to us in powerful ways through the Scriptures. We must pray each and every day of our lives—not only for ourselves but also for others—because prayer makes a difference.

MARRIAGE

Many of you would be surprised how much marriage counseling I do as a pastor. And I can promise you that it causes me great pain to see marriages fall apart both inside and outside of the church. But in the time that I have spent working with couples both before and after they are married, I have come to a few conclusions:

- *Marriage is not easy*. And if it is easy right now, it won't always be easy. But commitment is a choice that you make.
- *You must do everything in your power to put the needs of your spouse first*. If both spouses are doing this, then there is always someone looking out for your best interest.
- *Once you have children, don't neglect your marriage*. I've seen so many couples who once

What the World Needs Now

had healthy marriages; but when children came along, they started spending all of their time being mothers and fathers and they forgot their roles as husbands and wives. Take time to get away. Spend intentional time together and keep the flame alive so that your marriage stays healthy and strong through the years.

- *You must learn to communicate.* Most of the problems that arise in marriage are the result of one or both spouses failing to communicate and letting their spouse know how they feel. When communication starts to deteriorate, a marriage can get into trouble very quickly. In large part, the quality and consistency of the communication dictates the quality of the marriage.

FAMILY

This naturally goes hand in hand with marriage. In a simple life, family is a top priority. Parents, whether you realize it or not, your children look up to you and watch everything that you do. It doesn't matter how old you are or how old they are, so always try to set a good example. Young parents, be careful not to work too much because your children will grow up before you know it. The more time you spend with your children, the more love and care they will feel from you, and the better off they are going to be.

Also, rely on your family to support you if you can. No matter what happens in life, you will hopefully be able to turn to your family; family is meant to be where you are accepted no matter what—without any pretenses, without any conditions. Be the family member to your parents, brothers, sisters, and children that you want them to be to you.

SERVICE

I once heard it said that there is no smaller package than somebody all wrapped up in themselves. How true that is! Jesus said that he came "not to be served but to serve" (Matthew 20:28), and he calls us to do the same. We live in a world that can be very self-centered and self-focused, and the only way that is going to change is if we learn to serve other people. It starts with our families and grows from there. And it is only when you start serving others that you realize the joy that it brings in your own life.

BEING GRATEFUL

All of us have so many blessings in our lives, but all of us are also guilty of taking those blessings for granted. If we can spend our lives being thankful to God then we will be much happier and grateful people. If thanksgiving is a priority, then jealousy, envy, anxiety, and bitterness seem to melt away. No matter what is happening in your life right now, give thanks to God for the many blessings that you do have—because all of us are blessed in so many ways.

CHAPTER 30

Sabbath

For some reason, workaholism is rewarded in the United States. It's an idol, along with money, that we seem to rationalize away. In fact, it is often rewarded. What is not talked about nearly enough, though, is what can be sacrificed in the name of building a career and achieving success: the quality of a marriage, time with children, being home for dinner, spending time with friends, and so much else that brings lasting joy and fulfillment.

Perhaps it is because we tend to think of the United States as the land of opportunity, free enterprise, innovation, and entrepreneurship that we just don't want to call this out. But we should. Balance is always the key, yet so many people struggle to find that sacred balance. It is possible to work hard, be successful, and still make time for family and other things. In fact, it is absolutely essential for our long-term happiness to live a balanced life.

One of the things that I worry about in this overscheduled, overbooked, multitasking culture of ours is that we have lost the concept of Sabbath. At this time in our history, Sunday has become just another day, and many of us don't take the time to slow down, to rest, to be with our families, and to fill our own cup. Many people live exhausted from day to day, longing to recharge and catch a break.

Sabbath

As speaker and author Matthew Kelly writes in *The Rhythm of Life*: "The world is full of men and women who work too much, sleep too little, hardly ever exercise, eat poorly, and are always struggling or failing to find adequate time to spend with their families. We are in a perpetual hurry—constantly rushing from one activity to another, with little understanding of where all this activity is leading us."[1]

Modern parents find themselves in a constant rush—hurrying from work to school to day care to baseball to hockey to ballet to the doctor to church. College students, too—even those living a life of relative leisure—are always complaining about how busy they are and the stress and pressure they are under.

The world has gotten itself in an awful rush, to whose benefit I do not know. We are too busy for our own good. We need to slow down because this breakneck, no-rest lifestyle is destroying us.

In the Book of Genesis, at the very beginning of the Bible, we find the account of creation. God creates the heavens and the earth, the waters and the sky, the plants and the trees, the sun and the moon, the birds and the fish, the animals, then God creates human beings in God's own image. And on the seventh day, God blesses the work that has been done…and then rests. God rests! But many of us never rest. God, the all-powerful and all-knowing ruler of the universe, rested. But we don't rest.

Megan and I have three children. Our kids stay busy playing multiple sports, acting in school plays, going to dance and voice lessons, having slumber parties, and trying to not miss out on

What the World Needs Now

everything else that is happening around them. With both parents working full time, getting the kids to all the places they are supposed to be is quite a challenge. Modern families have managed to overschedule themselves to death. What this overscheduling does is keep us going and going to the point where we never seem to rest or have a break. We have a really hard time saying no because we don't want our kids to miss out. It's understandable, but at the same time, things weren't always this way. And we can learn how to dial it back and have more balanced schedules.

Learning to simplify our lives goes hand in hand with living our priorities and keeping a Sabbath. We can't do it all, even though many of us try. We can't let our kids do it all, even if that means that they might miss out. Learning to slow down the pace of life is a good thing. We should not be afraid of it. We have no excuse for not observing the Sabbath. We do so at our own peril. The Sabbath was made for humankind, not humankind for the Sabbath. Rest! Renew! Recharge! Discover the rhythm of life. Find a balance so you can enjoy life and be in the present.

Wayne Muller wrote a great book on this subject titled *Sabbath Rest: Restoring the Sacred Rhythm of Rest*, where he says, "For Jesus, rest is a precious ointment, a balm for the heavy heart. Jesus, for whom anything was possible, did not offer 'seven secret coping strategies' to get work done faster or 'nine spiritual stress management techniques' to enhance our effectiveness. Instead, he offered the simple practice of rest as a natural, nourishing, and essential companion to our work. Learn from me, he invited, and you will have rest for your souls."[2]

CONCLUSION
Why Character Matters

As this book prepares to go to press, I am approaching my forty-fifth birthday. Megan and I have now been married sixteen years, and our children will soon be fifteen, thirteen, and nine years old. I am completing my eighteenth year as senior minister of Woodmont Christian Church and my sixth year teaching at Vanderbilt University. For me, those things show that time really flies!

We all know that but how quickly we tend to forget. To return to David Brooks's metaphor, I certainly believe that I am now on my second mountain of life. I am highly focused on the things that matter most: faith, spiritual growth, family, deep friendships, meaning, and purpose. This saying, often attributed to Ernest Hemingway, helps orient me, especially when I feel discouraged: "There is nothing noble in being superior to your fellow man; true nobility is being superior to your former self." That is a great mantra to live by. We should all strive to improve ourselves, to reorient our lives toward what is truly most important, to think hard about the kind of person we want to be and the kind of lives we want to live. That is the spirit in which I offer the words in this book.

We all have our flaws. I certainly have mine. But there is a big difference between people who are always trying to improve

What the World Needs Now

and those who simply don't care, or even worse, those who don't feel like they actually have any work to do. My children are growing up in an age that is very different from the one I grew up in. They have iPhones, social media, Google, YouTube, and they always know what their friends are doing and what they might be missing out on. Parenting has never been easy, but the challenge has now reached new levels.

At the end of the day, however, I want my kids to understand why character will always matter. Character is who you are, not what you have. It's the way you treat the people who can do nothing for you in return. It's the values that you live by day in and day out. How you speak, act, and react. It is also closely tied to how we process our thoughts and emotions. In this book, I have tried to identify important values and why I think they are now more necessary than ever before. These values and virtues must be passed along to our children and grandchildren.

Life is full of choices, big and small. We make them every day. These choices include what to read, where to go, who to spend time with, who to listen to, and how to grow. As the result of our ongoing decisions, we are always being formed by many different factors and people. So, the real question has never been, Are we being formed into something? We are! Every single day and in every stage of life! Rather, we need to ask, What are we being formed by? Are we being formed by healthy or unhealthy factors, people, circumstances, and ideas? We make decisions every day that set the stage for who we are always already becoming. Then we have to live with the results of those decisions, both good and bad.

In my university courses, we talk a lot about the bigger picture of life. I challenge students to think ten, twenty, thirty years down the road. What kind of life do they want to build? What kind of person do they want to become and then marry? What type of career will they choose? What kind of friends will they have? The goal, ultimately, is to build a meaningful life in which they love, serve, give back, and know their values and priorities. Many decisions made along the way will be important. Setbacks will happen. Disappointments will surely come. But they must learn to press on and keep moving forward.

Life is not easy for anybody. Some have it much more difficult than others. I think about my friends Mike and Katy Dieckhaus, who lost their daughter Evelyn in the Covenant School shooting just down the street from our church. I can't even imagine the pain they feel walking into her empty bedroom, looking at an empty chair at the dining room table. Yet they have pressed on courageously with fortitude and resilience, and they are living their life with purpose and conviction. They are not giving up. People like that inspire me to do what I do. They have taken what life has handed them, bounced back, and found purpose amid heartache and strife.

Being a pastor of a large church and a university professor is a fascinating combination that keeps me very busy. I get to be with people in all different kinds of situations: joys, sorrows, weddings, funerals, births, baptisms, and graduations. I am

What the World Needs Now

there for the highs and the lows, the celebrations and when life falls apart. What I often see through all of this experience is that Viktor Frankl was absolutely right: we don't choose everything that happens to us, but we do choose if and how we will respond. Our attitude always matters. Obstacles can become opportunities. Who we are deep down will always shine through.

If our lives were to end tomorrow, are we satisfied with what we've done, how we have loved, and who we have become? That's a question worth asking.

NOTES

Introduction
1. Jonathan Sacks, *Morality: Restoring the Common Good in Divided Times* (New York: Basic Books, 2020), 1.
2. David Brooks, *The Second Mountain: The Quest for the Moral Life* (New York: Random House, 2019), xvi.
3. David Brooks, *The Second Mountain*, xxii.
4. David Brooks, *The Second Mountain*, xvi.

Chapter 1
1. Ben Sasse, *Them: Why We Hate Each Other and How to Heal* (New York: St. Martin's Press, 2018), 22–23.
2. Arthur Brooks, National Prayer Breakfast Keynote Address, Washington, DC, February 5, 2020.
3. Arthur Schopenhauer, *Essays and Aphorisms*, trans. R. J. Hollingdale (London/New York: Penguin Books, 2004), 170.

Chapter 3
1. "Resilience," American Psychological Association, accessed February 26, 2025, https://www.apa.org/topics/resilience.
2. Diane Coutu, "How Resilience Works," *Harvard Business Review* (May 2002), www.hbr.org/2002/05/how-resilience-works.
3. "Building Your Resilience," American Psychological Association, updated February 1, 2020, https://www.apa.org/topics/resilience-building-your-resilience.
4. David L. Moore, *The Liberating Power of Pain* (Saint Louis: Chalice Press, 1989), 16.

Chapter 4
1. Alain de Botton, *The School of Life: An Emotional Education* (London: The School of Life, 2020), 3.
2. Viktor Frankl, *Man's Search for Meaning* (Boston: Beacon Press, 1992), ix.
3. Augustine, *Confessions* (Oxford: Oxford University Press, 1992), 3.
4. Daniel Goleman, *Emotional Intelligence: Why It Can Matter More than IQ* (New York: Bantam, 1995), 33–111.

Chapter 6
1. Harold Kushner, *Overcoming Life's Disappointments* (New York: Anchor Books, 2006), 41.

Chapter 7
1. Serene Jones, *Call It Grace: Finding Meaning in a Fractured World* (New York: Viking, 2019), xvi.

Chapter 8
1. Timothy J. Penny, "Facts Are Facts," *National Review*, September 4, 2003, https://www.nationalreview.com/2003/09/facts-are-facts-timothy-j-penny/.

Notes

2 Ralph Waldo Emerson, *The Works of Ralph Waldo Emerson: Comprising His Essays, Lectures, Poems, and Orations in Three Volumes*, Vol. III (London: William Clowes and Sons), 219

3 Henry David Thoreau, *The Writings of Henry David Thoreau* (Walden Edition), (Boston and New York: Houghton Mifflin and Company), 364.

Chapter 9

1 Arthur Brooks, *Love Your Enemies: How Decent People Can Save America from the Culture of Contempt* (New York: Broadside Books, 2019).

2 Sacks, *Morality*, 216.

Chapter 10

1 F. Washington Jarvis, *With Love and Prayers: A Headmaster Speaks to the Next Generation* (Jaffrey, NH: David R. Godine, 2000), 251.

2 Kathryn Schulz, *Being Wrong: Adventures in the Margin of Error* (New York, Harper Collins, 2010), 42.

3 Jarvis, *With Love and Prayers*, 257.

Chapter 11

1 Michael Curry, *Love Is the Way: Holding on to Hope in Troubling Times* (New York: Avery, 2020), 9.

2 Curry, *Love Is the Way*, 19.

3 Curry, *Love Is the Way*, 27.

Chapter 12

1 David Brooks, *The Road to Character* (New York: Random House, 2015), 262–263.

2 Thomas Keating, *The Contemplative Journey*, Vol. 1, tape 1, Sounds True, 1997, cassette, quoted in Rita DeMaria and MoTherese Hannad, eds. *Building Intimate Relationships: Bridging Treatment, Education, and Enrichment through the PAIRS Program* (New York: Brunner-Routledge, 2003), 175.

Chapter 13

1 Stanley Hauerwas, *The Peaceable Kingdom: A Primer in Christian Ethics* (South Bend, IN: University of Notre Dame Press, 1991), 47.

Chapter 14

1 Thich Nhat Hanh, *The Art of Living* (New York: HarperCollins, 2016), 177.

2 Jerry Sittser, *A Grace Disguised: How the Soul Grows through Loss* (Grand Rapids, MI: Zondervan, 1995), 48.

Chapter 15

1 Gerard Baker, "How American Institutions Went from Trust to Bust," *Wall Street Journal*, September 8, 2023, https://www.wsj.com/articles/american-institutions-went-from-trust-to-bust-media-schools-business-promises-43c8d18.

2 Baker, "How American Institutions Went from Trust to Bust."

Chapter 16

1 Daryl Austin, "Divorce Rates Are Trickier to Pin Down than You May Think. Here's Why," *USA Today*, September 5, 2024, https://www.usatoday.com/story/life/health-wellness/2024/09/05/marriage-divorce-rate/74899214007/.

Notes

Chapter 17

1 C. H. Spurgeon, *Everybody's Book: The Pilgrim's Guide, A Word for All Times and All Seasons* (London: Passmore & Alabaster, 1897), 51

Chapter 18

1 Johann Hari, *Lost Connections: Uncovering the Real Causes of Depression—and the Unexpected Solutions* (New York: Bloomsbury, 2018), 89.
2 Hari, *Lost Connections*, 99.

Chapter 19

1 George E. Vaillant, *Triumphs of Experiences: The Men of the Harvard Grant Study* (Cambridge, MA: Belknap Press, 2015).
2 Stanley Hauerwas and William Willimon, *The Truth about God: The Ten Commandments in Christian Life* (Nashville: Abingdon Press, 1999), 130.

Chapter 20

1 Sacks, *Morality*, 215.
2 Sacks, *Morality*, 216–219.

Chapter 21

1 F. Washington Jarvis, *With Love and Prayers*, 309.
2 Edwin H. Friedman, *A Failure of Nerve: Leadership in the Age of the Quick Fix* (New York: Church Publishing, 2017).

Chapter 22

1 Joshua Brown, "The Nine Financiers: A Parable about Power," *Forbes*, July 25, 2012.
2 Tim Keller, *Counterfeit Gods: The Empty Promises of Money, Sex, and Power and the Only Hope that Matters* (New York: Dutton, 2009), 51.

Chapter 25

1 Mike Slaughter, Charles E. Gutenson, Robert P. Jones, *Hijacked: Responding to the Church Partisan Divide* (Nashville: Abingdon Press, 2012), 42.
2 Slaughter, Gutenson, and Jones, *Hijacked*, 42.
3 Jonathan Haidt, *The Happiness Hypothesis: Finding Modern Truth in Ancient Wisdom* (New York: Basic Books, 2006), 242.

Chapter 26

1 Steven R. Covey, *The Seven Habits of Highly Effective People: Powerful Lessons in Personal Change* (New York: Golden Books, 1997).
2 John Mark Comer, *Practicing the Way: Be with Jesus. Become like him. Do as he did.* (Colorado Springs: Waterbrook, 2024), 77.

Chapter 27

1 John C. Maxwell, *How Successful People Lead: Taking Your Influence to the Next Level* (New York: Center Street, 2013).

Notes

2 Rick Warren, *The Purpose Driven Life: What on Earth Am I Here For?* (Grand Rapids, MI: Zondervan, 2002), 21.

Chapter 30

1 Matthew Kelly, *The Rhythm of Life: Living Every Day with Passion & Purpose* (New York: Fireside, 2004), 147.
2 Wayne Muller, *Sabbath Rest: Restoring the Sacred Rhythm of Rest* (New York: Bantam, 1999), 24.